Japan and the California Problem

Japan
and
The California Problem

By

T. Iyenaga, Ph.D.
**Professorial Lecturer in the Department of Political Science,
University of Chicago**

and

Kenoske Sato, M.A.
Formerly Fellow in the University of Chicago

G. P. Putnam's Sons
New York and London
The Knickerbocker Press
1921

Copyright 1921
by
G. P. Putnam's Sons

Printed in the United States of America

CONTENTS

CHAPTER I

INTRODUCTORY 3

CHAPTER II

JAPANESE TRAITS AND PHILOSOPHY OF LIFE . 9

Emotional Nature—Æsthetic Temperament—Group Consciousness—Adaptable Disposition—Spirit of Proletarian Chivalry—Philosophy of Life—New Turn in Thought.

CHAPTER III

JAPAN'S ASIATIC POLICY 33

Korean Situation—Policy of Self-Preservation—Shantung Settlement—Coöperation with China—Understanding with America—Japan's Proper Sphere of Activity.

CHAPTER IV

BACKGROUND OF JAPANESE EMIGRATION . 50

Causes of Emigration and Immigration—Japan's Land Area—Agriculture—Population—Industry—Social Factors.

CHAPTER V

ATTEMPTS AT EMIGRATION: RESULTS . . 64

Australia—Canada—South America—The United States—Results.

PAGE

CHAPTER VI

CAUSES OF ANTI-JAPANESE AGITATION .   .   75

Modern Civilization — Various Attitudes Towards
Japanese—Psychological Nature of the Cause—
Chinese Agitation Inherited — Local Politics —
"Yellow Peril"—Propaganda—Racial Difference
—Japanese Nationality—Modern Nationalism—
Congestion in California—Fear and Envy Incited
by Japanese Progress—Summary.

CHAPTER VII

FACTS ABOUT THE JAPANESE IN CALIFORNIA—
POPULATION AND BIRTH RATE .   .   .   90

Number of Japanese in California—Immigration—
"Gentlemen's Agreement" — Smuggling — Birth
Rate—What we May Expect in the Future.

CHAPTER VIII

FACTS ABOUT THE JAPANESE IN CALIFORNIA—
FARMERS AND ALIEN LAND LAWS .   .   120

History of Japanese Agriculture in California—Causes
of Progress — Japanese Farm Labor — Japanese
Farmers—Anti-Alien Land Laws—Land Laws of
Japan—Effect of the Initiative Bill.

CHAPTER IX

ASSIMILATION   148

Nationalism and Assimilation—Meaning of "Assimilation"—Biological Assimilation—Is Assimilation
without Intermarriage Possible?—Cultural Assimilation—Assimilability of Japanese Immigrants
—Native-Born Japanese.

CHAPTER X

GENERAL CONCLUSION   178

Contents

APPENDIXES

PAGE

APPENDIX A 198

Charts on Comparative Height and Weight of American, Japanese-American, and Japanese Children.

APPENDIX B 201

Extracts from the Treaty of Commerce and Navigation and Protocol between Japan and the United States of America, of February 21, 1911.

APPENDIX C 204

California's Alien Land Law, Approved May 19, 1913.

APPENDIX D 207

Alien Land Law, Adopted November 2, 1920.

APPENDIX E 216

Crops Raised by Japanese and their Acreage.

APPENDIX F 217

Japanese Immigration to the United States.

APPENDIX G 218

Japanese Admitted into Continental United States; Arrivals and Departures.

APPENDIX H 218

Immigrants and Non-Immigrants.

APPENDIX I 219

Distribution of Japanese and Chinese Population in the United States.

APPENDIX J 220

Distribution of Japanese in the United States, According to the Consular Division, as Reported by Foreign Department, Japan.

PAGE

APPENDIX K 221
   An Abstract of Expatriation Law of Japan.

APPENDIX L 223
   A Minute of Hearing at Seattle, Washington, before
   the House Sub-Committee on Immigration and
   Naturalization.

APPENDIX M 230
   Comparative Standing of Intelligence and Behavior
   of American-born Japanese Children and American
   Children Discussed by Several Principals of Elementary Schools of Los Angeles, California.

LITERATURE ON THE SUBJECT . . . 238

INDEX 247

NOTE TO ACCOMPANY THE SECOND EDITION

THAT the first edition of this book was exhausted in so short a time indicates the keenness of general interest in the vital issue of the Japanese problem in California.

There are some additions which the authors wished to make had there been time to do so, but because of the necessity of printing the second edition at once, they must be withheld for the time being.

During the short interval which has elapsed since the publishing of the book, events have developed in the Western States which clearly reflect the influence of California's example and the increasing seriousness of the problem. Legislation similar to the Alien Land Law voted on by the California electorate on November 2, 1920, has, in one form or another, been adopted or made the subject of deliberation by the Legislatures or State Constitutional Conventions of Arizona, Arkansas, Delaware, Louisiana, Nebraska, Nevada,

New Mexico, Oregon, Utah, and Washington. We believe, however, that none of these developments necessitates any alteration in the main position which we have taken in the book. They seem rather to strengthen our contentions by concrete facts. We are more and more impressed with the urgency of a right understanding of the situation and the formulation of a sane and sound opinion by the American people at large with regard to the vexing question.

T. I.
K. S.

NEW YORK, May, 1921.

Japan and the California Problem

Japan and
The California Problem

CHAPTER I

INTRODUCTORY

WHEN, during the middle years of the last century, thousands of stalwart pioneers moved westward to California in quest of gold, they had no idea whatsoever of the part of destiny they were playing. When, synchronously with that movement, Commodore Perry crossed the Pacific and forced open the doors of Japan with the prime object of securing safe anchorage, water, and provisions for the daring American schooners then busily engaged in trade with China, he never dreamed of the tremendous result which he was thereby bringing about. What those men were doing unconsciously was nothing short of preparing the way for contact and ultimate harmonious progress of two great branches of mankind and civilization which originally sprang from a common root, but which in the course of thousands of years of independent development have come to possess strikingly different characteristics.

Culture is aggressive and masculine; it craves conquest and vaunts victory. Once let loose in the open field of the Pacific, the East and West are now involved in a mighty tournament, the outcome of which is yet beyond mortal imagination. The most we can hope for is the speedy realization of Kipling's vision:

> But there is neither East nor West,
>   Border, nor Breed, nor Birth,
> When two strong men stand face to face,
>   Though they come from the ends of the
>   earth.

The Oriental problems in California, originating as they did in the conflict of local, economic, and political interests, have in recent years come to assume more and more the character of cultural and racial questions. The forms and motives of the movement for the exclusion of the Orientals are vastly diverse, often counteracting and contradictory, but deep in the bottom of the whirl there lies the fundamental question of race and civilization. To say the least, the present unrest in California with reference to the Japanese problem is the intensified, miniature form of the general struggle in which East and West are now being involved. Says Governor Stephens of California in his letter to Secretary of State Colby:

California stands as an outpost on the western edge of Occidental civilization. Her people are the sons or the followers of the Argonauts who wended their way westward . . . and here, without themselves recognizing it at the time, they took the farthest westward step that the white men can take. From our shores roll the waters of the Pacific. From our coast the mind's eye takes its gaze and sees on the other shores of that great ocean the teeming millions of the Orient, with its institutions running their roots into the most venerable antiquity, its own inherited philosophy and standards of life, its own peculiar races and colors.

This being the case, the magnitude of the Japanese problem in California can hardly be exaggerated. Enveloped in a state under the guise of local conflict, the problem is, nevertheless, a gigantic one, involving vital questions of world destiny. Shall the races of Asia and Europe, brought together by the progress of science, be once more strictly separated? Cannot different races, while remaining biologically distinct, form together the strong factors of a unified nation? Should white races organize in defense of themselves against "the rising tide of color" and invoke race war of an unprecedented scale and consequence? Is it not possible to arrive at some principle by which the contact of white and yellow races may be rendered a source of human happiness instead of being a cause for all the evil consequences imaginable? These are some of the questions which are contained in the Asiatic problem in California.

Already a considerable quantity of literature has appeared which sounds an extremely pessimistic forecast of the future of Eurasiatic relationship. Some writers erroneously divide mankind into so many races by the color of the skin, as if each were a pure, homogeneous race, and they indulge in the risky speculation of "inevitable" race war between the white race, which hitherto held supremacy, and the yellow race, which is now attaining a position of serious rivalry. Others urge the imperative need of organizing the white nations into a supernational state in order to enable them to weather the threatened attacks from the yellow races. All these arguments are based on the presumption that the Asiatic races wherever they go—in Australia, Canada, or America —create conflict with the Aryan race. The fallacy of such arguments lies in envisaging the large problem of East and West from its partial expression. The anti-Asiatic movement in the new world is certainly a significant problem, but it is only an incidental and local phenomenon of the great process under way of cultural unification.

That the California problem is not all that is involved in the relationship of Asia and America can readily be seen by the incessant increase, in spite of it, of close coöperation between them. In science, in art, in religion, in ideals, in industry, and commerce, and, last but not least, in sentiment, the peoples of these continents find themselves ever more closely bound together, learning to appreciate the inestimable value thereby created, and fast widening the scope of their group consciousness so as to embrace all mankind, thus concretely vindicating the futility of the idle speculation of race war based on the mere difference of skin pigmentation.

If the error of race-war theory arises from absorption in parts, overlooking their relations with the whole—from magnifying out of proportion the local racial conflict to the extent of eclipsing the value and significance of vastly more important relations—it behooves us to avoid such grievous mistakes and to view the situation in a broader perspective. Indeed, the key to the understanding and the solution of the difficulty of the Pacific Coast is in viewing it in the light of friendship and coöperation between America and Japan. Then, and only then, does it become clear how important it is to approach the problem with prudence and foresight, and to endeavor to solve it in a spirit of fairness and justice. It then becomes plain, in the face of the vastly important tasks involved in wisely conducting the relationship of Orient and Occident, how foolish and cowardly it is to assume a negative attitude of fear and withdrawal from the natural circumstance which time has brought about. Whether one likes it or not, the world is already made one, and any human attempt to divide it into air-tight compartments is hopeless. We are bound to have yet closer contacts among all races and nations. The way to a satisfactory solution of the California problem clearly lies in a closer and more intimate association—in a word, better mutual understanding between Orientals and Occidentals.

Let us then honestly seek to comprehend the heart of the difficulty and frankly discuss the question, untrammeled by any bias, prepossessions, or fear; with eyes steadily fixed on the larger aspects of the problem; eager to arrive at some constructive principles of solution satisfactory to all concerned.

CHAPTER II

JAPANESE TRAITS AND PHILOSOPHY OF LIFE

THE national traits of different peoples are, like our faces, similar in rough outline but infinitely different in the finer details. The people of Japan are in the larger characteristics not different from any other people; they are part of the aggregate of human beings and they possess all the instincts and desires which are common to humanity. But, as distinguished from other peoples, they display certain individual characteristics which are the product of a unique environment and history.

Emotional Nature.

Perhaps the most prominent characteristic of the Japanese is their excitable, emotional nature, which among the ignorant is often expressed in turbulent and irascible action, and which among the refined takes the form of a fine sentimentality and temperamental delicacy. This is rather the direct opposite of the American disposition, which

9

is stable, blunt and big, hearty and generous. Such difference is greatly responsible for mutual misunderstandings, such as the Japanese charge that the American is discourteous and inconsiderate, and the American impression that the Japanese is dissimulating, not to say tricky.

The emotional temper of the Japanese has played a large rôle in their history and constitutes a conspicuous factor in their national life. If the history of the Anglo-Saxons is primarily a story of competition and struggle for the control of power and the pursuit of material interests, that of the Japanese is a drama of sentimental entanglement largely removed from material issues. Without due regard to the rôle played by emotion, the history of the Japanese people is wholly incomprehensible. What, for instance, incited Hideyoshi to invade Korea in 1592? What made the Japanese accept so readily the teachings of the Jesuit Fathers during the latter half of the sixteenth century? What more recently induced Japan to insist at the Paris Conference on recognition of racial equality by the League of Nations?

If the emotionalism of the race has been deeply influential in the historic drama, it has been no less persuasive in the political and social life of the present-day Japan. Compare the Constitutions of America and Japan. If the outstanding features of the American Constitution are the safeguarding of the interests and rights of the individual, the states, and the nation, those of the Japanese Constitution are the expressions of the people's anxiety to recognize and perpetuate their beloved head, the Emperor, as the great, the divine ruler of their ideals. Although the onslaught of material-ism has wrought some changes in recent years, there yet remains the ineradicable proof of Jap-anese emotionalism in the realm of marriage and love, where all earthly considerations are forgotten, if not tabooed, and in the realms of family and of society, where the relations between parents and children, and between friends and neighbors, are conducted with an assured sense of devotion, love, and good will. The same tendency is to be rec-ognized in almost all Japanese institutions, educational, military, and political, while it is particularly true in the realm of æsthetics, includ-ing, art, literature, and music—a realm that is ruled by sentiment.

In the common daily life of the Japanese their emotionalism expresses itself in almost infinitely diverse ways. Their peculiarly strong sense of pride and dignity, individual, family, and national, a sense for which the Japanese will make any sacrifice, comes from their highly-strung nervous system. Their keen sense of pride gives rise to another marked Japanese peculiarity—an excessive susceptibility to the opinions and feelings of their fellow men. Social ostracism to the Japanese is a punishment which is often more unbearable than the death penalty. The peculiarly high rate of suicides in Japan is explained by statisticians as being largely due to some mistake or sin for which the offender would rather die than be chastised by society. The cold-blooded *hara kiri* was an institution by which the Samurai could sustain his honor or save his face when involved in disgrace. High-spirited temper, suppressed by ethical teachings, social conventions, and rigorous discipline, results in a singular contrast between external physical expressions and internal feelings. The placid faces, reserved manners, and reticence are but masks of the intense, burning spirit, whose spontaneous expression has been inhibited by centuries of stoic training. It is most unfortunate that this virtue in the Oriental sense has frequently been a cause of misunderstanding, making the Japanese appear dissimulating, and, therefore, untrustworthy.

But at heart the Japanese are neither as inscrutable or deceitful as some believe, nor are they as intriguing or profound as these terms would imply. They are kind and sympathetic, easily moved by the attitude of others, quite simple-minded and honest, lacking tenacity, audacity, iron will, or cold deliberation. In these respects, as in many others, the Japanese possess some of the weaker traits of the South European peoples. They have proved heretofore not a great people, but a little people "who are great in little things and little in great things."

The simple explanation of Japanese sentimentalism may be found in one of the original race stocks which migrated from southern islands of tropical climate, where emotion rather than will guides the conduct of the people. The topographical and climatic conditions of Japan have also had their influence, and these, with the numerous volcanic eruptions, frequent earthquakes, and recurrent typhoons, have given the people the disposition of restlessness and excitement. Perhaps also the social system of the Middle Ages, which was unduly autocratic and despotic, irritated the lower classes, driving them to turbulent and "peppery" conduct.

Æsthetic Temperament.

The next characteristic of the Islander is one which is closely related to the preceding trait. It is artistic temperament. Some scholars of archæology attempted to trace this characteristic to the original settlers of the empire, but the resultant opinions are so diverse as to deny scientific validity. Some of them maintain that the Ainu, the earliest known settlers in Japan, a now dwindling race living in the northern island called Hokkaido, were originally a very artistic people, contributing much to the æsthetic temperament of the Japanese. There are other scholars who insist that the Yamato race, and not the Ainu, was the most artistic, while there are still others who uphold the view that it was the vast horde of migrators coming from Korea, Tartary, and China who brought with them the love of beauty. But these are speculations of prehistorical conditions which are largely hidden from us by the veil of mythology. What we can be sure of is that the influence on the people of the exceptionally beautiful natural surroundings reflected itself in their artistic genius. Encouragement of art and literature and of artistic productions generally through the patronage of aristocrats, who enjoyed from the earlier ages leisure and wealth, has also had much to do in making the Japanese artistic.

What influence has this æsthetic temperament exerted on the life of the Japanese? In the first place, it has rendered Japanese civilization markedly feminine. This is shown by the fact that the creative efforts of the people were mainly directed to personal and home decoration and to literary and artistic pursuits, instead of to masculine efforts to fight and conquer the forces of nature, from which alone the sciences are born. Particularly noticeable was the almost total absence of science in Japan, in striking contrast to the remarkable wealth of art at the time, some half a century ago, when the country began a critical introspection of itself in comparison with other nations.

In the second place, it had the effect of making the people inclined to underestimate the value of material things and to exaggerate the glory of the spiritual aspects of life. This is most clearly seen in the teachings of Bushido,[1] which laid strong emphasis on the baseness of the conduct that has for its motive pecuniary or material interests, and which taught the subordination of the body to the soul as the most essential virtue of the Samurai. The traditional custom of sacrificing the material side of a question for the satisfaction and uphold-ing of the emotional side still survives in present Japan, and constitutes one of the marked charac-teristics of the Japanese. His strong inclination towards imagination, meditation, and religious belief is too well known a fact to require more than a mention here.

It seems true that people gifted æsthetically are more apt to turn hedonistic. While it remains

[1] *The System of Samurai Ethics and Obligations of Honor.*

doubtful whether the Japanese are more immoral than other peoples, as is so frequently charged, it is quite true that they take more delight in a leisurely comfort of living, going to picnics, attending theaters, calling upon friends, and holding various ceremonies and feasts. Generally speaking, although not given to excesses, they show no puritanic disposition about drink and are lavish spenders for luxuries. In the tea houses and other places of social amusement they spend money often beyond the reasonable proportion of their income. They are not a thrifty people.

Group Consciousness.

Next to the artistic disposition must be mentioned their strong group consciousness. It is true that all people have a certain degree of group consciousness which emerges out of the facts of common biological and cultural heritage and experience. But in the case of the Japanese this group spirit is markedly strong, expressing itself in loyalty and patriotism. Most strangely, the spirit of *Yamato*, or the Japanese group spirit, has had its source more than anywhere else in primitive myths. Two ancient books of mythology, *Kojiki* and *Nihongi*, record the story of the Japanese ancestors who were originally born of the gods of heaven and earth, and who settled in Japan and

established there through their brave deeds the
majesty of the Empire of Nippon. From these
ancestors sprang the people of Japan. This myth
is faithfully believed by the Japanese, and the
people worship at the shrines where the spirits of
their heroic ancestors are supposed still to reside
and guard the country. So strong is this belief in
the myth even to-day that, in spite of the anthropological discovery that the original settlers of the
island were of diverse races and possessed no advanced culture, the people still cling to the idea
that the Japanese are a pure and glorious race,
having sprung from one line of ancestors which was
divine and which is now represented by its direct
descendant, the Emperor.

In addition to mythology, what bound the
Japanese so close together was the natural environment and the lack of cosmopolitan associations.
Marooned as they were on little islands, the mutual
association and intermarriage of people took place
freely, and in the course of time established a sub-
stantially complete homogeneity of the population.
The internal unity was further strengthened by
the policy of national seclusion, which gave the
common people the idea that Japan was the only
universe and that the Japanese were the only
people on earth. In modern times, the group spirit
or patriotism has been skillfully encouraged and

2

enkindled by utilizing the national experience of the wars with China and Russia, and by a system of education which aimed to impress on the minds of children the glory of their people and history, the absolute duty of being loyal to the Emperor, and the hostile tendency of foreign countries toward their own.

What the people gain by narrow patriotism in the maintenance of national integrity they lose in their failure to take a broad view of things. This stubbornly obstructs the Japanese in their efforts to view their country in its proper relation to other countries; it hinders them from being "Romans when in Rome"; it makes the idea of following the example of England, the policy of loose national expansion, wholly unthinkable—Japanese colonies must be exclusively Japanese. The chief cause of the failure of Japanese colonization and emigration must be attributed to the strong consciousness of the Yamato Minzoku (Yamato race). This has made the Japanese noticeably narrow-minded, quite awkward in their relations with different peoples, and more or less given to race prejudice. The reputation of the Japanese as poor mixers is well known. Their strong race prejudice has been exemplified by their attitude toward the Chinese, Koreans, and the outcast class of their fellow countrymen, called *Eta,* which has been nothing short of prejudicial discrimination.

In spite of the desperate efforts of the militarists and bureaucrats to conserve narrow patriotism and racial pride, it has been found increasingly difficult to do so, since the facts and thoughts of the West became accessible to the people. When the marvelous scientific achievements of the Occidental peoples, their advanced political and social systems, their profound philosophies of life and of the universe, together with their superior physique and formidable armament, were appreciated, it became all too apparent, even to the most conceited mind, that the culture and racial stock, in which the Japanese had taken so much pride, were sadly inferior, and that years of hard toil would be necessary before they could be the equals of the Occidentals. The pathetic cry of Japan for recognition of racial equality by the League of Nations is a reluctant admission of this fact.

The outcome of this disillusionment has been the appearance of three currents of thought with reference to the national policy. One is the ultra Occidentalism which sees nothing good in their own country and people, and hence is extremely merciless and outspoken in denunciation of things Japanese, but which admires even to the point of worship almost everything that is European and

American. To this school belong many younger radicals who are more or less socialistically inclined and who would like to see Japan converted into a republic or a Bolshevik communism. Categorically opposed to this thought is another school, which its adherents call "Japanism." This school sees nothing new or worth while in things Occidental, and advocates, after the reasoning of Rousseau, a return to natural Japan. Between these two extremes stand the majority of sane intellectuals, who clearly perceive both the limitations and the strength of Japan, and endeavor to benefit through learning and assimilating the valuable experience of advanced nations.

Adaptable Disposition.

Another notable feature of the Japanese is their meager endowment of originality and, conversely, their marked aptitude for adaptability. A glance at the outline of Japanese history shows how much the Japanese borrowed from other peoples in almost all phases of civilization and how little they themselves have created. Indeed, there is hardly anything which belongs to Japan that cannot be traced originally to the earnest creative effort of other peoples. The same may be said of modern peoples, who, with the exception of scientific inventions, have mainly derived their culture from the Greeks and Romans. Whatever difference the future may witness, the Japanese thus far have been borrowers and receivers of other races' accomplishments. Perhaps this is the cause of the rapid development of the Japanese, who have succeeded in imitating and assimilating the strong points of nations in succession from the lower to the top of the hierarchy—from Korea, China, India, to Europe. When the process reaches the top of the ladder, let us hope that Nippon will start for the first time real creative work.

Spirit of Proletarian Chivalry.

The discussion of Japanese traits would be very incomplete if we omitted one outstanding idiosyncrasy that has not yet been mentioned. So peculiar is this trait to the Japanese that there is no adequate word to designate it in other languages. The Japanese express it by such words as *kikotsu*, *otokodate*, and *gikyoshin*. The nearest English equivalents for these terms would be heroism and chivalry. It is a mixed sentiment of rebellion against bully power, sympathy for the helpless, and willingness to sacrifice self for the sake of those who have done kind acts. This admirable sentiment must be strictly distinguished from the spirit of Bushido, because it has arisen among the plebeians in place of Bushido, which was the way of the Samurai or aristocrats, although it may have been, as some scholars claim, the source of inspiration for the growth of proletarian chivalry.   Bushido has found an able propounder in Dr. Nitobé.   Under the Tokugawa régime the Samurai was the flower and the rest were nothing.   The Samurai often abused their privilege and oppressed the common people not a little, disregarding their rights and personality. Then a class of plebeians appeared who called themselves "men of men," and who made it their profession to defy the bullying Samurai and to defend the oppressed people.   It was the virtue of this class always to help the weak and crush the strong, and to be ready to lay down their lives at any moment.   The story of Sakura Sogoro, who fell a martyr to the cause of oppressed peasants, has become a classic.

Thus originating in defiance of despotism, the spirit of proletarian chivalry permeated among the lower classes of people, and to this day it forms the bulwark of the rights and freedom of the common people.   Refined and enriched by the embodiment in it of enlightened knowledge and ideals, the sentiment came to be on one side a keen appreciation of kindness and sympathy, and on the other a strong hatred of oppression and injustice.   The present proletarian movement in

Japan, a movement which is destined presently to become a mighty social force, owes its source and guidance to "the ways of the common people."

If Dr. Nitobé is right in predicting that Bushido, "the way of the Samurai," will eventually enjoy the glory of "blessing mankind with the perfume with which it will enrich life," we may reasonably hope that proletarian chivalry will succeed in bringing about general freedom and democracy in Nippon, in defiance of military and imperialistic domination.

The understanding of this trait of the common people of Japan goes far to explain what has puzzled those Americans who wonder why the Japanese immigrants in this country are so unsubmissive and rebellious. In his letter to the Legislature of Nevada, the late Senator Newlands stated: "The presence of the Chinese, who are patient and submissive, would not create as many complications as the presence of Japanese, whose strong and virile qualities would constitute additional factors of difficulty." Governor Stephens of California, too, observes in his letter to the Secretary of State: "The Japanese, be it said to their credit, are not a servile or docile stock." Acquired by centuries of opposition to arbitrary power, the trait has become almost instinctive, and expresses itself even under democracy whenever they think they are unjustly treated.

In discussing the features of Japanese character thus far, we have taken care to state the known causes which gave rise to each trait. This has been done with a view to preparing ourselves to answer the question; To what extent are these characteristics of the Japanese inherent in the race and to what extent acquired? The answer which the foregoing discussion suggests is that they are both inherent and acquired, biological and social. While racial stock is responsible to an extent, other factors, such as natural environment and social conditions, have helped to develop the characteristics of the Japanese. Perhaps the best criterion by which we can determine the relative strength of heredity and environment in this case is to observe how and in what respects the Japanese, born and reared in other countries, undergo transformation in their mentality and characteristics. We shall touch on this point again later when we discuss the characteristics of the American-born Japanese children.

Philosophy of Life.

It is but natural that the philosophy of a nation developed from the life and experience of people should be deeply colored by their temperament.

After having discussed the essential features of the Japanese disposition, it may be easy to anticipate the character of philosophy which rests on it. We shall now consider the outstanding features of Japanese thought, with a view to interpreting and evaluating the spiritual side of Japan's civilization.

True to the characteristics of the Japanese, who lack initiative, the thought of the people also manifests a marked absence of originality. Until, in the early part of the sixth century, Buddhism and Confucianism came into the country, the Japanese seem to have had no system of religion or philosophy save fetichism and mythology. The advent of new doctrines of ethics and religion caused a rapid transformation of the life and ideas of the people, elevating them by one stroke from barbarian obscurity to civilized enlightenment. From this time on a childish admiration of mythological characters and stories began to be superseded by an earnest effort for the perfection of the individual character and the realization of social ideals; and crude superstitions were gradually replaced by the profound teachings of Gautama. Out of the religious zeal were developed admirable art and literature, and from the moral effort were born elaborate ethical codes, social order, and social etiquette. Thus, with raw materials imported, the Japanese worked diligently and carefully to turn out finished products well adapted to their tastes and needs. If the Japanese were people endowed with great originality, they would surely have given evidence of it during nearly three hundred years of national seclusion (1570–1868), when almost all conditions requisite for a creative impulse were present, including peace, prosperity, need, and encouragement. In fact, however, the people were interested and absorbed in stamping out the feeble hold of Christian influence, in assimilating the teachings of Wang Yang Ming, and in recasting the doctrines of Confucius and Buddha. When the flood gates of Japan were thrown open and the tides of Occidental learning swept in, the Japanese were almost overwhelmed, and found themselves too busy in coping with them to think of the original contribution.

Lack of ability to start new things is generally compensated by the capacity to borrow new things. In the point of borrowing new ideas and then working these to suit their own tastes, the Japanese are probably second to no nation on earth. Japan first borrowed Confucianism and Buddhism, and within a short time remodeled them in ways peculiar to her, rendering their identity with the original almost unrecognizable. Thus the stoic, pessimistic character of Buddhism was greatly modified, becoming more or less epicurean and optimistic in the hands of the Japanese. The casuistic, practical, individualistic ethics of Confucius were radically changed to general principles of ideal conduct, with the addition of æsthetic elements, and a strong emphasis laid on group loyalty rather than on filial piety. It is to this ability of the Japanese to assimilate new thought and new belief that the unexpected success of early Catholic propaganda was chiefly due. To this capacity of assimilation is also due the origin of Bushido, which is essentially an eclectic of Confucian, Taoist, and Buddhist doctrines. The later-day Shintoism, the so-called cult of ancestor worship, is also a product of the skillful combination of native mythology, Taoism, and Confucianism, with an infusion of certain of the Buddhist doctrines. That the present Japanese civilization is largely a product of assimilation by native genius of American, French, German, and English ideas and institutions is an established fact. It may be that therein lies the hope, as many Japanese thinkers cherish, of making Japan a modern Alexandria, where centuries of human achievements in Asia and Europe may be harmoniously woven together for the realization of a more perfect fabric of civilization.

In literature it is asserted that the creative period is uncritical and the critical period is barren.

It seems that the critical tendency is the anti-thesis of creative effort. This applies to the Japanese, who do not create but who are keenly critical. Instinctively bent on absorbing new ideas, they immediately react to any new schools of thought—turning from Eucken to Bergson, again to Russell, now to Einstein—but they soon begin to analyze their doctrines and to find fault and fallacy here and there, and, finally, are ready to depreciate them wholesale. In so doing, of course, they assimilate some of the good points involved in various systems. The chief obstacle which Christianity, as interpreted by healthy-minded missionaries, encounters in Nippon is the sceptical temper of the Japanese intellectuals.

A strong appeal to emotionalism and to the sense of beauty rather than to cold reason and un-pleasant realities is another common characteristic of Japanese philosophy. The Japanese have always taken pride in expressing great truths in a short verse form called *Uta*, with choice words and exquisite phrases. Until the advent of European learning, poetry and philosophy were never clearly distinguished in Japan. Love of emotionalism naturally leads Japanese thought to humanism rather than to metaphysical speculation.

From this it may be thought that English positivism would find great vogue in Japan. In fact, the influence of Adam Smith, Bentham, Mill, Malthus, and others was a considerable factor in shaping modern Japanese thought. But at bottom the Japanese are not utilitarians. They are by temper idealists. The magical power by which German idealism as propounded by Kant, Hegel, and Fichte, and more recently by Lotze and Eucken, controls the Japanese mind is astounding. Nearly all the prominent philosophers of the Meiji era may be classed under some branch of German idealism. The fact that of American thinkers Emerson is more widely read than any other, and that Royce is more popular than James, is no accident. If pragmatism appeals to the Japanese mind, it is not in the logical form of Professor Dewey but rather in the æsthetic presentation of Santayana.

New Turn in Thought.

Recently, however, or more particularly since the war, the trend of Japanese thought has began to follow a somewhat different path. Industrial revolution, which has been rapidly advancing during the past twenty years, reached its culmination during the war, when various forces accidently combined in bringing about universal recognition of the need for radical social reorganization. Capitalism, which had in the course of

time grown to be a gigantic power, proved unable
to adapt itself to the changing conditions of the
day, and it thus obstructed the onward march of
liberalism and democracy. Labor, however,
shook off the dust of long humiliation, and began
with united front to demand recognition of its
rights and of humanity. The struggle naturally
forced the attention of the people to the actual
condition of society, where the poor majority are
sadly left in destitution, where sins and crime are
sapping the very vitality of the people, where the
rich are abusing their fortunes for deplorable
ends. Then came the European downfall of autoc-
racy and the triumph (at least for a short time) of
democracy. Liberty, equality, and fraternity
became once more the slogan of the time. All these
forces united and started a reform movement,
upsetting to a certain degree the age-long social
system of Nippon.

The three years of confusion did a lasting good.
The German systems of government, diplomacy,
education, military affairs, and philosophy, to
which the Japanese had hitherto adhered too
blindly, were, one after another, filtrated and
purified, thereby removing much of the scum that
was in them. It is, of course, impossible for hard-
ened militarists and bureaucrats to get rid of the
beliefs in which they were born and brought up

and which have become endeared; but the old generations are gradually dying off, carrying with them to the grave the skeleton of systems which are now dead. In open rebellion against these falling autocrats there arose a great number of brilliant young people, bred and trained in the new school of liberty and democracy, with courage and foresight to complete the second Restoration— that of the rights of humanity belonging to the common masses. Already the status of the working classes is greatly improved through a persistent, costly struggle against the misused power of capital; wages have been increased, hours shortened, and, in the near future, we may expect the triumph of industrial democracy, a triumph which will secure for labor the deserved right of industrial copartnership. Already the status of the women has been greatly improved by their emancipation from the traditional and social bondage under which they suffered so long. Political rights have been greatly enlarged, and universal manhood suffrage is now within view. The educational system, too, has just been revised, rendering its spirit a great deal more liberal than ever before. In this way, though the road is yet long and uncertain, true liberalism in Nippon at last stands firmly on its ground, ready to march towards its ordained goal.

Such a great social innovation is but a concrete expression of changes that are taking place in the underlying currents of thought. It indicates the breaking up of classic systems of moral and political philosophy, which by dint of age-long prestige had never ceased to exercise a strong influence upon the minds of the people. It discloses the bankruptcy of that German idealism which so precisely fitted in with the *à priori*, passive, spiritual temper of the people but which proved hopeless in the face of vital problems of life and society. It means the exposure of the inadequacy of English utilitarianism, with its over-emphasis on individualism, to help the people effectually to solve many difficulties of society. The changes now taking place in Japanese thought imply the failure of those philosophies which belittle the value of the material, slight the position of mankind in the universe and fail to satisfy man's inherent craving for ceaseless progress. The new direction of Japanese thought is decidedly towards pragmatic humanism at its best, with due emphasis on the importance of the practical and social phases of life, enriched with the spirit of a sentimental delicacy and an æsthetic proclivity singularly characteristic of the people.

CHAPTER III

JAPAN'S ASIATIC POLICY

COLONEL THEODORE ROOSEVELT once remarked to one of the authors of this book, with his accustomed emphasis and gesture: "The United States' proper sphere is in this hemisphere; Japan's proper sphere is in Asia." With this text the great statesman was propounding an idea of deep political significance. What is suggested by the text is, of course, not that either of the two nations should resume its traditional policy of isolation or confine its activities within the specified zones, but rather it is to the effect that each should know its bounds and play the part which destiny and geography have assigned to it.

In further elucidating the same idea, in his book entitled *Fear God and Take Your Own Part,* Roosevelt says:

Japan's whole sea front, and her entire home maritime interest, bear on the Pacific; and of the other great nations of the earth the United States has the greatest proportion of her sea front on, and the greatest proportion of her interest in, the Pacific. But there is not the slightest real or necessary conflict of interests between Japan and the United States in the Pacific. When compared with each other, the interest of Japan is overwhelmingly Asiatic, that of the United States overwhelmingly American. Relatively to each other, one is dominant in Asia, the other in North America. Neither has any desire, nor any excuse for desiring, to acquire territory on the other's continent.

President Roosevelt had a unique opportunity of making himself thoroughly conversant with the situation in the Far East without even setting foot on the soil. The Portsmouth Treaty of 1905, the "Gentlemen's Agreement" of 1907, the Root-Takahira Agreement of 1908, negotiated on behalf of America by the able Secretary of State, Elihu Root, and the American recognition of the amalgamation of Korea into the Japanese Empire in 1910, are the outstanding acts of the Roosevelt administration wherein the foregoing idea has been translated into deeds. These acts have proceeded from a thorough appreciation of the history and development of modern Japan. Nor did Colonel Roosevelt cease on his return to private life to follow closely the march of events in Asia. He wrote many articles on Far Eastern affairs which showed his remarkable grasp of the situation. No wonder, then, that the Japanese people reciprocate this generous appreciation by paying the highest respect to, and entertaining a genuine admiration for, the late American statesman.

Korean Situation.

Recently Japan has been made the target of attack from many quarters with reference to her Asiatic policy. The Shantung settlement, the Korean administration, and Japan's activities in East Siberia have been severely assailed by her critics. Patriotism imposes upon a citizen no obligation to condone any mistakes and wrongs which his country has committed. We deplore the gross diplomatic blunder which Japan made in 1915 in her dealings with China, which, although perfectly justifiable in the main proposals presented,[1] had the appearance of browbeating her to submission by brandishing the sword. We deplore the atrocities perpetrated in the attempt to crush the Korean uprisings. Whatever may have been the advisability of adopting drastic measures to nip the Korean revolt in the bud, a revolt which, if leniently dealt with, might have resulted in far greater sufferings of the people, it can never be proffered as a plea for the committing of inhuman deeds. Fortunately, a change of heart has come to

[1] See "The New Chino-Japanese Treaties and Their Import," by T. Iyenaga, in *The American Review of Reviews*, September, 1915.

the Mikado's Government, which, by uprooting the militaristic régime, is now resolutely introducing liberal measures and reforms in Korea. The most significant of the measures is the system of local self-government which has just been inaugurated. It creates in the provinces, municipalities, and villages of Chosen (Korea) consultative or advisory Councils whose functions are to deliberate on the finances and other matters of public importance to the respective local bodies. The members are partly elective and partly appointive. Besides these deliberative Councils, there will be established in each municipality, county, and island a School Council to discuss matters relating to education. This is the sure road to complete self-government in Chosen. The same process of evolution, which brought local autonomy and a constitutional régime to Japan proper, which took thirty years to perfect, is now being applied to the newly joined integral part of the Mikado's Empire. The step may be slow, but the goal is sure. Korea's union with Japan was consummated after the bitter experience of two sanguinary wars and the mature deliberation of the best minds of the two peoples. Its revocation is out of the question, unless it is demanded in the future for most cogent reasons. The privilege of taking a hand in the government of the empire, however, should be extended as speedily as possible to its subjects in the peninsula.

Policy of Self-Preservation.

Many as are the pitfalls into which Japan has fallen in pursuance of her Asiatic policy, it may confidently be asserted that the road she has trodden has, on the whole, been straight. She can face with a clean conscience the verdict of history. When Far Eastern history, from the China-Japan War to the conclusion of the Versailles Treaty, is carefully examined and rightly understood, it will be conceded that the course which Japan has adopted, so far as its general principles are concerned, is the one which any nation of self-respect and right motive would pursue. Fundamentally Japan's Asiatic policy is the policy of self-preservation, the policy of defense, and never of aggression. The Anglo-Japanese Alliance, which was and still remains the cornerstone of Japan's Asiatic policy, was formed for purely defensive purposes, in order to maintain peace in Asia and safeguard mutual interests vested therein of the two Powers. Only the "inexorable march of events" has brought Japan into Korea, Manchuria, and East Siberia. None of the statesmen who took part in the Meiji Restoration could ever have dreamed that their country would in the course of time be driven through sheer force of circumstances to plant its flag on the Asiatic mainland. It was solely in self-defense that Japan took up arms against China and Russia. Once enmeshed in continental politics, however, it became imperative for her to take such measures as would ensure and consolidate the position and gains that were won through enormous sacrifice of blood and treasure. Herein, in short, is the genesis of Japan's present status in Korea and Manchuria.

Even at the present time, the heavy arming of Japan is a case of necessity, so long as the Far East remains in such an unstable condition as exists there to-day, and is not free from the menace of the Bolsheviki, who, professing pacifism, are not slow to emulate the military machine of Imperial Russia. Nothing could be more welcome to the Japanese people than to see the curtailment of their naval and military equipments, for the maintenance of which they have to bear the burden of crushing taxes, and to behold the day when they can, without fear of interference by force of arms, win their spurs in the Far East by engaging in the peaceful enterprises of farming, trade, and industry.

Precisely as the position of Japan on the Asiatic mainland was the result of arbitrament by the sword, drawn in response to a challenge made by others, and is now upheld by the prestige of arms, her Asiatic policy, although conceived in self-defense, came to assume in the eyes of the outside world a semblance of military aggrandizement. As a consequence, Japan is looked upon as a militaristic nation, bent upon conquest. Suspicion and fear are thereby engendered. This is, to say the least, extremely unfortunate. No stone should be left unturned to smooth the sharp edges cut by this historical retrospect and to obliterate the unpleasant memories of the past. No effort would be too great for Japan to convince the world of her genuine faith that her future lies "not in territorial and military conquest, but on the water in the carrying trade and on land in her commercial and industrial expansion abroad." Her erstwhile failure to dispel the suspicion of the world about her intentions and to take it into her confidence is the root of many ills with which she has been afflicted for the past few years.

Shantung Settlement.

The storm of criticism we have witnessed in America about the Shantung settlement is a good illustration. Whatever part party politics in the United States may have played in raising the furor, had Japan secured the complete confidence of the American people, all the eloquence expended for

the denunciation of the Shantung clause in the
Versailles Treaty would surely have fallen on deaf
ears. That our judgment is not wrong is sustained by the fact that the Portsmouth Treaty
evoked not a word of protest in America. We
need not remind our readers that the Treaty concluded through the good offices of President Roosevelt and the settlement made at Versailles are not
only based upon the same principles but are exactly
identical in many respects, with this most important exception—namely, that the former Treaty
transferred to Japan the lease of the Kwantung
territory, and she still holds it, while in the latter
case she pledges herself to relinquish the leasehold
of Kiaochow, thereby restoring the complete
sovereignty of China over Shantung, which had
been infringed upon by Germany. The Shantung
settlement is, consequently, of a far greater advantage to China. What Japan secures in that
province is only the same economic rights and
privileges which are enjoyed by other Powers in
other parts of China. There is, therefore, no justifiable ground for singling out Japan for attack
with regard to the international arrangement now
in vogue in China. Were the complete reconstruc-
tion of China, the re-writing of her history, to be
attempted, international justice would demand
that the parties interested should all share equal

responsibilities and sacrifices. Discrimination against Japan alone is unjust, unfair. The would-be builders of the new heaven and the new earth can ill afford to lay the cornerstone of their edifice on such an unsafe and unlevel ground. Manifestly, the dawn of the millennium is still far away. We have to make the best of the world as it is. To ignore this fact is to make the confusion in the world worse confounded. As a result of this misapprehension of history, the Shantung question still remains in abeyance, because of China's refusal to enter into negotiations with Japan for the restoration of Kiaochow, thus delaying perfect accord between the two Oriental neighbors whom destiny has called to be on the best of terms. The foregoing interpretation of the Shantung question could not in ordinary circumstances have failed to convince the practical American people of the appropriateness of the Versailles settlement, were they not tempted to indulge suspicions of Japan and, hence, ready to be easily misled by false stories, misrepresentations, and slanders concocted by her enemies.

Rather unfortunate, one is sometimes tempted to think, has been the heading of the clause in the Versailles Treaty, that has readjusted the German-China Treaty of 1898 and its sequel, and disposed of the rights and privileges Germany had secured thereby in the province of Shantung. Like "the

three R's" and other catchwords that have in
American history often proved so powerful in misleading the people, so this curt phrase "Shantung
clause," which was seized on and skillfully utilized
by Japan's critics, has been a cause of mountains
of misunderstanding that have crept into the
heads of the American people, who, as a rule,
take neither time nor pains to examine the subject
carefully and thoroughly. As a result, they imagine that the whole province of Shantung was
ceded to Japan by the Peace Treaty. Great,
indeed, as is this mistake, it would be extremely
difficult to correct it, as the mischief has already
been done, except by the actual restoration of
Kiaochow. Japan cannot, of course, be held
responsible for the misinterpretations of other
people, but at the same time it would be well for
her to spare no effort to convince China of the
wisdom of entering into negotiations for the re-
covery of the leased territory, and, consequently,
of her complete sovereignty over the province of
Shantung. Until this pledge is redeemed, Japan's
credit will suffer, and all her pronouncements on justice and humanity fall flat on the ears of the world.

Coöperation with China.

While Japan's Asiatic policy was, of course,
primarily formulated to further her own interests,

it has also been inspired with the laudable ambition of rendering a good record of stewardship over the people who have come within the orbit of its influence. No one who knows the work undertaken in Korea and South Manchuria will grudge a word of praise for the record. It has bestowed untold benefits on the inhabitants. Theodore Roosevelt, in reviewing the enterprise of Japan in Korea, grew enthusiastic over it. The same story is repeated in South Manchuria, where the South Manchurian Railroad Company, acting as a civilizing agent, has wrought marvels. We should like to dwell here with patriotic pride on these reforms and undertakings in some detail, were they not out of place in this book.

Commendable as are these civilizing measures adopted by Japan, the fact remains that she has signally failed in one great essential, namely, in winning the good will and friendship of her neighbors. This is the weakest spot in the armor of her Asiatic policy. She is thereby jeopardizing her future. The sentiment of good will is as much a fact, though imponderable, as any other fact, and is a force of immense consequence. How vital this moral asset is to Japan can easily be gauged when we consider that in her neighboring lands are found the indispensable materials for her industrial expansion and the best market for her commerce.

Japanese leaders are thoroughly aware of the importance of this moral asset, and have done all that they could to secure it.

The failure to win it is partly due to the pettiness of Japanese officialdom, so bitterly complained of by Lafcadio Hearn with his fine poetical irony— the pettiness which tries to bring everything within its prescribed order and does not allow free play to the idiosyncrasies and peculiar characteristics of other peoples. No less responsible are the shortsightedness of Japanese nationals, their too great eagerness to accomplish things within a short time, their haughtiness and overbearing manners, which are decidedly offensive to their neighbors. The fault, however, is not Japan's alone. There are tremendous difficulties which confront her in the way of winning the friendship of her neighbors. The first to reckon with are their weak and unstable qualities, which have so sadly but too clearly been shown by their incapacity to organize a strong nation or to put their house in order. To deal with these neighbors is no easy task. It requires the highest statesmanship. The task is made difficult a hundredfold by the counteracting influences exerted on Japan's neighbors, as they are in the vortex of international rivalry. And not all foreigners are the friends of Japan. There is a considerable number of those who enter-

tain, for one reason or another, a dislike of the
Island Empire, and ceaselessly labor to defeat its
purpose. They paint, either wittingly or unwittingly, every act of Japan so maliciously that it
instills fear and hatred of her among her neighbors.
Undiscriminating and unfair attacks of Japan's
critics play into the hands of the jingoistic elements in the countries concerned and make the
task of the liberals extremely difficult. Whatever
the obstacles, however, they must be surmounted,
for the future road to tread is clear. Japan's
salvation, together with that of her neighbors, lies
in their genuine friendship and coöperation.

Understanding with America.

A brief review of Japan's Asiatic policy was
deemed advisable in connection with the discussion of the Japanese-California problem in order to
see how Japan proposes to solve the question of
human congestion at home and to meet her other
urgent needs. The succeeding chapters will show
what an unparalleled predicament Japan is facing.
Circumscribed within a narrowly limited area, only
16 per cent. of which is fit for cultivation, and
crowded with two thirds as many people as the
entire population of the United States, with an
annual increase at the rate of seven hundred thousand, Japan must perforce find a way whereby her

people may live contentedly and develop robustly. Emigration and industrial expansion are manifestly the exits from the dilemma of slow strangulation. Emigration, however, is found a difficult exit, for the Japanese find themselves barred from the most favorably placed lands of the earth. Australia, Canada, and the United States, with their vast lands yet sparsely peopled, and their immense resources left unexploited, while welcoming every race and creed of Europe, shut their doors against the Japanese.

Japan has acquiesced without much ado in the restrictive immigration measures adopted by America and by British colonies from the higher consideration of international comity. She saw that there lies at the bottom of these measures the delicate question of race difference, which requires a long period for its proper adjustment. To ignore this fact and force the race issue, however just in principle, would be to court disaster. It might result in the loss of friendship of her best associates in international affairs and of the vital interests involved in that friendship. At the same time, the "Gentlemen's Agreement" which Japan has entered into is evidence of her sincere solicitude to avoid embarrassment of her friends by the influx of an alien race. It is then but just that they reciprocate the courtesy by a sympathetic understanding of Japan's difficulties.

Barred in the east and south, it is natural for Japan to strive to find room and employment for the surplus of her population in her neighboring lands—the sparsely peopled Manchuria, Mongolia, and East Siberia. Climate, cheap and efficient native labor, and the unfavorable economic conditions, however, preclude the immigration in large numbers of Japanese laborers into these regions. Only by building up large plants and inaugurating big agricultural enterprises, in cooperation with the natives, could Japan hope to transplant in these lands some portion of her skilled laborers and traders. During the stay of a decade and a half in South Manchuria, limited as it was until the conclusion of the China-Japan Treaties of 1915 to the Kwantung territory and the railway zones, Japan can count therein as colonists only a little over 150,000 of her sons and daughters.[1]

The only alternative which remains and which is the most feasible proposition to absorb the energies of her crowded population is found in her

[1] According to the result of the census taken on October 1, 1920, the Japanese population of South Manchuria stands at 154,- 998 souls. Of this total, those living at Dairen number 63,745; Fushun, 12,659; Mukden, 12,268; Port Arthur, 9379; Antung, 7057, and Anshan, 6678, while those resident in the jurisdiction of Kwantung Province number 74,893.

commercial and industrial expansion.   Here again, however, she is terribly handicapped, as we shall see in the next chapter, by the conspicuous absence and scarcity of raw materials indispensable for industrial development.   Fortunately, in the territories of her neighbors—China and East Siberia—there are vast stores of these materials untouched and unused, the unfolding of which will not only meet her wants, but will equally benefit her neighbors.   The supreme importance of winning their good will thereby becomes accentuated a thousandfold, for without their willing coöperation nothing can be accomplished.   In the participation of the benefits accruing from the development of her neighbors' natural resources Japan need not ask for special privileges.   The faithful and effective execution of the "open door" policy is all she requires.   Here she stands on common ground with Occidental Powers.   She entertains no fear of the outcome of the "open door" policy, for she is in a position to secure every advantage accruing from its operation.

Japan's Proper Sphere of Activity.

As Colonel Roosevelt pointed out, "Japan's proper sphere is in Asia," and it is but proper that her activities therein develop in intensity and vigor.   She is entitled to use every peaceful and legitimate means that is open to her for the extension of her influence in the Far East, for it is there that she can assure herself of her right to live. America and Great Britain, while reserving to themselves the right of opening or closing their own doors to the Japanese, will not be playing a fair and even game if they grudge to recognize this fact. In the strict adherence on the part of Japan to the spirit which gave birth to the "Gentlemen's Agreement," and in the just appreciation on the part of America of Japan's difficulties at home and abroad, lies one of the fundamentals of an equitable solution of the Japanese-California problem.

4

CHAPTER IV

Causes of Emigration and Immigration.

DIVERSE as are the causes that induce emigration and invite immigration, the most fundamental of all, with the exception of a few extraordinary cases, such as that of the Pilgrim Fathers, is economic pressure. There is a close relationship—a mutual give and take—between the immigrants and those who receive them. Generally speaking, human activities have their main-spring in man's desire to improve his conditions of living. The motive which induces the people of one country to go out and settle in another country is the same as the motive which induces another people to invite immigrants from other countries. True, in the former case, the direct reason for the move is generally the over-crowding and poor natural environment at home. In the latter case, it is the lack of man-power and the presence of great unexploited natural resources. But in both cases the real motive is the pursuit of interest, which may be reciprocally

promoted by the transaction. It is well to keep
this point clearly in mind at the outset, because
much of the confusion in discussing the Japanese
problem in California arises from forgetting the
real cause which brought Japanese immigrants to
America and which induced America to invite
them.

During the early colonial period the American
colonies invited refugees from political and religious
oppression to come and settle in the new world of
freedom and democracy. The remnant of this
early spirit still remains embodied in the present
immigration laws of the United States. Nevertheless, it is almost a dead letter, with great historic
interest but with no practical significance. The
real motive for welcoming immigrants has been
the acquisition of man-power for the exploitation
of vast natural resources and for the development
of industry. This is a fact which may be observed
in almost all "new worlds," including the South
American republics, Canada, and Australia, where
the dearth of human energy is the capital reason of
slow economic development. With settlers, however, the economic motive is not the only one,
though it is predominant. Here the motives are
diverse and complicated. With the Japanese
there are particular causes which have been driving
them to seek opportunities in new worlds.

Japan's Land Area.

The first and foremost cause is Japan's limited and unresourceful land. The land area of Japan Proper is 147,655 square miles, which is about 8,000 square miles less than that of California. The terrain of Japan is mountainous and volcanic, being traversed by two chains of mountains. One runs down from Saghalien towards the center of Honshu and the other from China via Formosa headed towards the north, both meeting at the middle of Honshu, thereby producing rugged upheavals popularly known as "the Japanese Alps." Being thus rocky and mountainous, the area contains a very small portion of plain land. Hokkaido, the extreme northern island, has seven plains. Honshu, the main island, has between the mountains five small plains, and Kyushu, the large southern island, has one. The total area of plains forms about one fourth of the entire area of Japan. The consequence of this geological formation is that about 16 per cent. of the total area is fit for cultivation, while over 70 per cent. of it is made up of mountains and forests.

Agriculture.

The Japanese having always been primarily farmers, agriculture still remains the principal occupation of the people. More than half the

population is earning a livelihood wholly or partially by agricultural pursuits. The large number
of farmers and the small amount of agricultural
land allotted to them has given rise to the most
intensive cultivation, which probably has no
parallel in the world. Nearly five and a half
million families, or thirty million people, cultivate
fifteen million acres, which means less than three
acres per family, and half an acre per individual
farmer. It is little wonder that the law of diminishing return has long been operating, rendering the
agricultural pursuit less and less remunerative,
driving farm hands to industry and other work.
The average daily wage of the farm laborer was
56 sen in 1917, while that of the industrial laborer
was 1 yen.[1]

In recent years the Government undertook a
thorough examination of the tillable land in the
country and reported as a result that there is yet a
possibility of reclaiming about five million acres.
By way of experiment, the Government began,
with the approval of the 41st Session of the Diet
(1918–19), to undertake the work of partial rec-
lamation of seven hundred thousand acres on a
nine-year program, with an outlay of some four
million yen. It is yet uncertain how the enterprise
will turn out; but it is fairly doubtful, in view of the

[1] One dollar U. S. currency is approximately two yen.

fact that already the land is utilized almost to the limit of cultivation, including narrow back yards and rugged hillsides, as well as sandy beach, whether the program can materially increase the present amount of farm acreage.

Parallel with the effort to extend the tillable land, everything has been done to increase the productivity of the soil under cultivation. Thanks to the application of scientific methods in agriculture and the use of fertilizer, the average yield of all crops per acre has increased since 1894 by about 35 per cent. But experts assert that owing to the excessive employment of land the soil now indicates signs of exhaustion, and that accordingly any further increase of productivity cannot be hoped for. On the contrary, the tendency will be toward a gradual decrease of productivity in the future. This is a grave forecast for Japan, and makes that country dependent more and more upon the food supply from abroad. The average yield of staple crops in Japan during the past few years comprises: barley, nine million koku (a koku is approximately five bushels); rye, seven million koku; wheat, five million koku; millet, four million koku, and rice, the most important crop, fifty-two million koku. The crops are far from being sufficient to feed a population of fifty-five millions, and Japan buys annually millions of koku of staple food from abroad. Taking rice, for instance, the average annual consumption is fifty-eight million koku, which exceeds by six million koku the average annual yield of Japan, so that the deficiency is made up by imports from Korea, China, and India.

Naturally, the Japanese, being very good farmers and fond of agriculture, and yet having so small a prospect of success at home, look with eager eyes for an opportunity to cultivate land abroad. In the north there are the vast plains of Manchuria; towards the south the fertile soil of Australia; in the east, California and Hawaii appear to offer golden opportunities for industrious farmers. Manchuria, however, turned out to be too cold, and competition there with cheap Chinese labor proved unprofitable. Australia, from the beginning, never welcomed the yellow races. Only Hawaii and California seemed in all respects satisfactory for Japanese emigration. Hence, large numbers of Japanese farmers migrated to these places during the years between 1891 and 1907.

Population.

Another big factor of Japanese emigration is the overcrowded status of the home population. Strangely, during the three centuries of national isolation, Japan's population remained fairly static, varying only slightly around twenty-six millions. A reasonable explanation of this peculiar phenomenon may be found in the rigid social structure of feudalism, which allowed no swelling of population beyond a certain number. Malthusian factors, such as pestilence and famine, as well as artificial means of control, operated in effectively thwarting the increasing forces of population.

When, however, feudalism was at last destroyed and in its place were established new forms of political and social systems which were much more liberal and advanced, the population suddenly began to swell at a tremendous rate. The advent of Occidental enlightenment which went far to improve the economic conditions of the country, and hence the conditions of living among the people, greatly encouraged the rapid multiplication of the number of people. Within the last fifty years the population of Japan has nearly doubled, increasing from thirty millions to fifty-five millions. At the present time the population is increasing at the rate of 650,000 to 700,000 per annum within Japan proper alone. The census taken on October 1, 1920, shows the total population of the Mikado's Empire as totalling 77,005,510, of which that of Japan proper is 55,961,140.

The significance of Japan's population cannot be

appreciated unless it is considered in connection with her land. The total area of Japan proper we have seen to be 147,655 square miles and the population close to 56,000,000. That is to say, the number of inhabitants per square mile is 380. This is rather a high figure when compared with that of other countries. Germany with her dense population counted, in 1915, 319 per square mile; France had 191, America 31 (1910), India and China, famous for density, had populations enumerated respectively at 158 and 100. Great Britain has rather a dense population (370 per square mile), but she has vast colonies, the population of which is extremely thin. This comparison of the number of people per square mile does not tell the true story until the quality and resources of each square mile are also compared. It has already been made clear that only 16 per cent., or fifteen million acres, of the land of Japan proper is tillable. This gives only one quarter of an acre of agricultural land per capita of population. In Great Britain agricultural land occupies 77 per cent. of the total area; in Italy, 76 per cent.; in France, 70 per cent. and in Germany 65 per cent.

Industry.

Handicapped as she is in agriculture, and holding on the other hand a vast and ever-increasing population, the best, in fact the only, policy for Japan to follow has been to utilize her vast man-power for the development of industry. Firmly convinced that the future of Japan depends solely on her ability to stand in the world as an industrial nation, the far-sighted statesmen of Japan long ago formulated plans for a steady industrial expansion. These plans were furthered by Government subsidy and have been faithfully carried out step by step by the authorities. The creation of a vast merchant marine; the building of railroads throughout the country, closely knitting all parts of the empire together; the enactment of a care-fully drafted protective tariff; the national and municipal monopolization of public utilities and important industries; the establishment of a stable financial system with facilities for financing healthy enterprises; the establishment of technical schools throughout the empire for the training of experts and skilled workmen, and thousands of other re-markable undertakings were accomplished within a very short time by the direct and indirect efforts of the State.

The people, too, were not behind in their devo-tion to the cause of making Japan an industrial power. They toiled most willingly under all kinds of disadvantages and hardships; they shouldered extortionate taxes with smiling faces; they worked

in unison, disregarding for the time being petty
private interests; they calmly and bravely met all
privations and adversities. There is little wonder
indeed that Japan established herself within only
a few decades as an industrial nation of the first
rank.

In order to get a general idea of Japan's industrial strides, a few figures will perhaps suffice.
Take, for instance, the number of factories. There
was not one factory, properly so-called, in the
country at the time of the Restoration in 1868; as
late as 1885 there were but 496 industrial companies, joint stock or partnership, with a total
capital of seven million yen. In the year 1900,
however, there were 7000 typically modern factories, and this number rapidly multiplied, subsequently reaching over 25,000, with billions of
paid-up capital. The number of factory operatives,
too, correspondingly multiplied during that period.
Less than 500,000 twenty years ago, they now total
1,500,000. The increase in the output of production and multiplication of various kinds of industries has been particularly phenomenal. In the
textile industry the production has increased more
than 300 per cent. during the past twenty
years, cotton yarn having increased from
30,000,000 kan (one kan is approximately equal
to 8.27 pounds avoirdupois) in 1900 to 100,000,000

kan; and in the silk textiles from 2,500,000 kan to
7,500,000 kan. In cloth fabrics, similarly the value
turned out in silk weaving increased from $42,000,-
000 to $100,000,000; in cotton weaving from
$30,000,000 to $200,000,000 between the years
mentioned. The corresponding increase of output
has been realized in almost all established industries, and the same ratio obtains in the many new
industries which have sprung up in recent years.
Generally speaking, the industry of Japan, which
was established on a firm footing by the year 1900,
has trebled during the last twenty years.

The World War, too, by absorbing for military
purposes all the energies of the belligerent Powers
in Europe and America, was greatly instrumental
in stimulating the industrial growth of Japan, who,
after accomplishing her allotted task at the initial
stage of the great conflict, was thereafter called
upon by her Allies to do her utmost in supplying
their urgent needs in ships and industrial products.

The development of industry naturally accom-
panies a similar expansion in commerce. The
total amount of foreign trade, which started with
the meager sum of $13,000,000 in 1868, jumped
to about $250,000,000 in 1900, and in 1920 reached
$2,124,000,000. That is, within the past twenty
years only, Japan's foreign trade increased roughly
ten times, and during the past fifty years 163 times.

Yet, with all this remarkable development, the future of Japanese manufactures does not allow unqualified optimism. In several important respects the foundation of Japan's industrialism is seriously hampered. In the first place, the supply of raw material is pitifully meager. With the exception of silk, Japan has in store hardly any raw material worthy of mention. She produces no wool or cotton and has only a limited store of iron. With the exception of coal, in which alone she is fairly independent—at least for the present— Japan depends for these indispensable factors of modern industry mostly on foreign supply. Scarcity of iron, in particular, is a notable weakness of Japan as an industrial nation.

The many mistakes Japan made in her labor policy, which were the inevitable outcome of the extreme difficulty she confronted in adjusting the sudden transition from the Feudal régime to the modern industrial stage, must also be counted as a cause in retarding the progress of her industry. Due to exceedingly low wages, long working hours, and lack of adequate protection of labor from exploitation, the man-power of Japan has been greatly lavished and wasted. The paternal social systems inherited from the feudal days long refused to allow the voice of the working classes to be heard and to give them freedom to improve their status. Strikes and labor unions, whatever their motive and character, have always been frowned upon in Japan. It is by no means too much to say that the present development of Japan's industry has been achieved largely by the costly sacrifice of health and the rights of millions of laboring men and women. Considering how costly was the present achievement of industry, there remains some doubt as to how far Japan can carry on its progress in the future.

It may seem that the development of industry must have brought a marked improvement in the standard of living of the masses. Such, however, is not the case. It has indeed immensely swelled the pockets of plutocrats, but has not much benefited the rank and file. While the income of the lower classes has not increased to any large extent, the cost of living has gone up by leaps and bounds, aggravating the severity of their struggle.

When both farming and manufacturing failed successfully to cope with the ever-increasing population, the only alternative for the Japanese was emigration. Among the students, the talk of another alternative, namely birth-control, is becoming a fad.

Social Factors.

Besides the economic reasons so far discussed there are social reasons which induce Japanese youths to go abroad. Socially an old country like Japan contains a vast accumulated crust of custom and tradition which refuses to adapt itself to the changing conditions and ideals of the age, and which, therefore, is objectionable to the younger generation who know something of the value of freedom and democracy. Again, the national conscription for military service is becoming increasingly distasteful to the youths of individualistic inclination. It is but natural, in the face of such powerful and numerous fetters which obstruct the free development of lives and personalities, that the young people of Nippon should seek opportunities abroad.

All these factors above described would not have constituted the effective motive forces for Japanese emigration had it not been for the assumed external advantages. Attractive narratives in which some of the new countries, more especially America, were represented as places where economic opportunities are really boundless and where an ideal state of freedom and democracy prevails, took an exaggerated form in the imagination. The glaring contrast which the visualized America presents with the actual Japan stimulates the desire of young men to turn to America and try their fortunes.

CHAPTER V

ATTEMPTS AT EMIGRATION: RESULTS

THE history of Japanese emigration began only a few decades ago. Immediately after the conclusion of treaties with the Western Powers many Japanese youths were sent abroad to acquire advanced Occidental knowledge. A number of adventurous persons and travelers also knocked at the doors of western countries, but they were not immigrants. Real immigration movement did not start until the facts of other countries became more or less known; until the colossal task of economic and social "revolutions" was well started; until the influence of European imperialism began to take root in the empire. Then came a brief period of "emigration fever" towards the end of the eighties, lasting some twenty years. What follows is a brief history of the various attempts made by Japanese to emigrate into different countries, and the results of the experiment.

Australia.

Because of the geographical proximity and alluring temptations that the vast uncultivated lands and rich natural resources presented, Australia was the place which early attracted the Japanese. A few hundreds of them began to migrate to several colonies, chiefly to Queensland, New South Wales, and Victoria. But they soon found the conditions exceedingly uncomfortable, owing to the hostile feeling already prevalent there against the Asiatics. The Australian fear of an influx of Asiatic races was early aroused by Chinese immigrants, who, as early as 1848, attained a sufficient number to cause agitation and race riots in several colonies. These colonies subsequently enacted rigorous anti-Asiatic immigration laws restricting the number of immigrants admitted per annum to a few hundred. Since then, filled with the fear, real or imaginary, of a menace of Asiatic inundation from across the equator, where one-half of the planet's population live congested on one-tenth of the total area of the earth, the great task of Australia during the last sixty years has been to keep the country clear of Asiatics.

The immigration policy of the Commonwealth of Australia presents perhaps the most clear-cut and radical example of racial discrimination. While, on the one side, she spares neither effort nor money to attract and welcome white settlers, on the other side she leaves no stone unturned to exclude all Asiatic immigrants. With an im-

mensely large area—about 50,000 square miles
more extensive than that of the United States—
yet almost untouched, and a population less than
that of the City of New York, Australia really
needs farmers, artisans, and all other classes of
people. It is the function of the Commonwealth
Department of Home and Territories to advertise
in Europe, through lectures, films, exhibitions, and
posters, for the purpose of inviting laborers and
settlers to Australia. Each State of the Commonwealth has extended assistance in money and
privilege to hundreds of thousands of European
immigrants. The cause for lamentation by the
government is that with all this effort and sacrifice
she has not been successful in getting any considerable number of people as settlers.

Unsuccessful in attracting white settlers, she
has been most successful in repelling the yellow
race. She has an immigration law which requires
immigrants to pass a dictation test—a test in
writing of not less than fifty words of a European
language—which is dictated to them by an officer.
Examination in a European language for the
Asiatics! And what is more, the Europeans are
exempt from it. The law provides, furthermore,
that Asiatic immigrants may be required to pass
a test at any time within two years after they have
entered the Commonwealth. Even for the recep-

tion of those Asiatics who have been lawfully admitted, some of the States, New South Wales, Queensland, South Australia, and Tasmania in particular, do not allow them the right of owning or leasing land, under the pretext that they are not eligible to citizenship. The Commonwealth of Australia does not extend the right of naturalization to Asiatics. No wonder, then, that there is only a handful of Orientals in that vast country—35,000 Chinese and some 5000 Japanese.

Canada.

Until recent years, no record was kept of the number of Japanese immigrants arriving in Canada and consequently the development of the movement cannot be accurately traced. The Canadian census of 1901 shows that 4674 persons born in Japan were in the Dominion at that time; 4415 were in the Province of British Columbia, the rest being scattered in the Provinces of Manitoba, Saskatchewan, and Alberta. After that year the number of Japanese immigrants coming to Canada gradually increased, and when the United States placed restrictions on the influx of Japanese from Hawaii, and the latter began to seek entrance into Canada, the number grew considerably and soon caused serious concern to the people of Western Canada. It was estimated that in 1907 the Jap-

anese domiciled in Canada had reached eight
thousand. Determined opposition soon arose
among the western provinces, and protests were
sent by the Canadian Government to Hawaii and
Tokyo requesting them to control the sudden
immigration tide. An agreement was reached in
1908 between Japan and Canada by which the
number of passports to be granted in any one year
to Japanese emigrating to Canada was limited to
four hundred. In this way the question was
satisfactorily settled.

Canada's treatment of the Asiatic races lawfully
admitted has been marked by leniency. She has
extended to the Orientals the privilege of naturalization and of securing homesteads. Even in
British Columbia, the center of anti-Oriental agitation, the Japanese and Chinese are permitted to
conduct business and cultivate land on an equal
basis with British subjects in Canada. They may
own land, both urban and rural, and in provinces other than British Columbia they are entitled to voting privileges when naturalized; only
in that province the Orientals are not allowed
to cast ballots, though free to become citizens.
It is reported that there are 13,823 Japanese
residing in Canada to-day, engaged in fishing
and logging and sawmill industries, as well as in
agriculture.

South America.

For some years past a number (about six thousand) of Japanese immigrants has been sent every year to Brazil in compliance with the request of the Republic. They have been mostly engaged on coffee plantations in Sao Paulo. The colonization is still in an experimental stage, and it is a little premature to forecast its future at this time. Altogether about twenty thousand Japanese immigrants have gone to the South American Republic.

The United States.

Perhaps attracted by the wonderful stories of the discovery of gold in the Sacramento Valley, or possibly cast ashore in boats on the Pacific Coast of America, there seem to have lived in the early sixties in California about a hundred Japanese. Early California papers record the story of quaint-looking Japanese settlers, who were received with great favor. Although accurate records are lacking, it would seem that the number of Japanese did not begin to increase until the late eighties, when a few hundred began to come in every year. The census of 1890 reported the number of Japanese residents as 2039. From that time on the number of immigrants steadily increased, reaching the highest mark in 1907, when about ten thousand of them entered continental America in one year.[1]

The direct incentive for Japanese emigration was furnished by a few large emigration companies,[2] which were formed with a view to supplying contract labor to Hawaii and America, where the demand for labor was insatiable. In the former case, the rapid growth of the sugar plantations demanded a large supply of cheap labor. In the latter case, the need for cheap labor was urgent, due to the enactment of the Chinese Exclusion Law in 1882, which soon began to effect a decrease in the number of Chinese laborers, resulting in a dearth of labor on the farms and in railroad work. It was in response to the urgent demand of capitalists and landowners in Hawaii and America for Japanese labor that the emigration companies sprang into existence with the object of facilitating the complex process of immigration.

The Japanese coolies so brought in were welcomed and prosperous—at least for a while. Their industry and frugality won them the confidence of their employers. In agriculture, in railroad-building, in mining and fishing, they proved useful

[1] For a complete tabulation of Japanese immigration see appendix F.

[2] Tokyo Emigration Co., Toyo Emigration Co., were the most conspicuous.

hands. They saved money and remitted to their native country a considerable portion of it. Some of them returned home with a fortune and a degree of refinement which a superior environment could bestow upon a laborer. These incidents stimulated the desire of ambitious Japanese to leave for and work in California and Hawaii, and the number of applicants for emigration greatly multiplied.

In the meantime, between 1895 and 1900, changes had taken place in the attitude of the people of California toward the Japanese. For various reasons the friendly feeling of the Californians was gradually replaced by a more or less hostile sentiment. It so happened that just about this time California was the stage for a struggle between organized labor and capital. It was with a great deal of effort and sacrifice that the organized labor of California succeeded in excluding the Chinese coolies. But their hard-won victory was shattered to pieces by the advent of Japanese laborers, whom capital, taking advantage of their ignorance of American customs and language, wisely utilized as a powerful weapon to defeat the unions. To the union men it made no difference whether the strike-breakers were Chinese or Japanese; whether strike-breaking was voluntarily or unwittingly performed; they were enemies just the same. The cry for exclusion was a natural consequence.

Then there also seems to be some truth in the report[1] made in 1908 by W. L. Mackenzie King, the Deputy Minister of the Government of Canada, which states that it is suspected that much of the anti-Japanese agitation in California was deliberately fermented by the interests of the Planters' Association of Honolulu, who, alarmed by the tendency of Japanese laborers engaged on the sugar plantations to seek work on the Pacific Coast of America, where wages were much better, started a campaign to check the exodus by causing ill feeling toward the Japanese along the Pacific Coast. The report states in part·

It is believed . . . that the members of the Asiatic Exclusion League in San Francisco were not without contributions from the Association's incidental expense fund, to assist them in an agitation which by excluding Japanese from the mainland would confine that class of labor to the islands, to the greater economic advantage of the members of the Association.[2]

For these two chief reasons, and perhaps for many other minor ones, there arose the persistent social movement for Japanese exclusion in Cali-

[1] Report of the Royal Commission appointed to inquire into the methods by which Oriental laborers were induced to come to Canada in 1909.

[2] Report as cited, p. 54.

fornia, which first took definite shape in 1900,
when a mass-meeting held at San Francisco
for the express purpose of more rigidly excluding the Chinese, adopted a resolution urging
Congress to take measures for the total exclusion of Japanese other than members of the
Diplomatic Staff. Following this came the first
of the anti-Japanese messages delivered by the
Governor of California, and of the resolutions
voted on by the State Legislature calling upon
Congress to extend the Chinese Exclusion Law to
other Asiatics. The climax of the movement was
reached when, immediately after the earthquake,
the Board of Education of San Francisco passed
the "separate school order," and Japan protested.
A series of diplomatic negotiations followed, which
finally resulted in the repeal of the school discriminatory order and the conclusion of the
"Gentlemen's Agreement," whereby Japan
pledged herself to restrict the number of immigrants to the United States.

Leaving to a later chapter the detailed discussion
of the result which the "Gentlemen's Agreement"
has brought about in the status of Japanese immigration, it will suffice to mention here that the
agreement has faithfully and loyally been carried
out by Japan, and that since then the Japanese problem has in fact ceased to be an immigration issue.

Results.

Twenty years of emigration attempts, chief of which we reviewed in this chapter, have resulted in failure in every case, and Japan's effort to plant her race in other lands has proved futile.   There are many causes for this failure, for which Japan is partially, but not wholly, responsible.   But this is a matter which we shall more fully discuss in the next chapter.   Excluded and maltreated wherever they went, the Japanese returned home with shattered hopes and wounded feelings, and the mooted question of population once more confronted them with intensified severity.   Giving up as entirely hopeless the attempt at settling in places where the white races held supremacy, they now appear to have made up their minds to migrate towards the north, where climatic and economic disadvantages, together with political revolution in Eastern Europe, have freed the land temporarily from the strong white grip, offering the line of least resistance for Japanese.

CHAPTER VI

CAUSES OF ANTI-JAPANESE AGITATION

Modern Civilization.

THE major cause of the agitation against Japanese in California must be attributed to modern civilization, which, with scientific devices, has conquered time and space and thereby destroyed the high walls of international boundaries. Indeed, had it not been for the steamboat, railroad, telegraph, and other civilized instruments, which bind the nations of the world into a composite whole, and modern industrialism, which civilization brought about and which in turn assisted in unifying the world, Japan for one would have remained a peaceful hermit nation, undisliked or unsuspected by any other. She, of course, has no reason to regret the adoption of European culture, which brought her untold values and happiness; but the fact remains that the present anti-Japanese agitation in California, as well as elsewhere in the world, would never have occurred had she not followed the lead of Occidental nations.

Clearly, such a conflict is one of the by-products

of the complex international relations brought about by modern science, which, simply because of the lack of experience and regulation due to their short history, remain deplorably defective. This suggests the point already brought out in our introduction, that the principle of the solution of the California problem lies not in an attempt at separating Japan and the United States, which time and destiny brought together, but in a yet closer, more regulated relationship, and in the promotion of a better mutual understanding.

Various Attitudes Towards Japanese.

With reference to the attitude toward the Japanese, it is possible to discern four classes of critics in California. There are the veteran exclusionists, whose only hope in this world seems to be the realization of the slogan, "All Japs must go!" There is the majority of people which is too preoccupied with its own affairs to investigate the facts and is ready to accept anything said or asserted by the exclusionists. Then there are those, intellectually more critical, who hold independent opinions as to why the Japanese must be excluded. There are also others who stoutly oppose, rationally or irrationally, any attempt at excluding the Japanese.

The reasons offered for justifying the exclusion

of the Japanese widely vary according to the class
of people, and they are often mutually contradictory and conflicting. To those agitators whose
motive is purely self-interest, agitation is a profession, and hence it transcends the consideration
of justice or international courtesy. They have
no scruples about lying or resorting to any means
which they think would serve their purpose. The
masses, generally speaking, accept what is given
to them by the agitators, unthinkingly echo their
voices, and so play directly into their hands.
Only fair, rational exclusionists study the facts
of the case, consider the significance involved
therein, and present arguments supporting their
conviction. It is in this class of people, and
not in professional agitators or whimsical populace, or irrational friends of the Japanese, that
the hope of the solution of the problem may
be found.

From the fact that so much agitation is going
on in California, some may think—especially
those in Japan—that all Californians are unkind or
hostile to the Japanese. This, however, is far from
being the case. It is precisely in California that
the most earnest, devoted friends of the island
people are found—found in great numbers.[1]

---

[1] Those who voted in the negative for the initiative bill were
222,086 against 668,483 in the affirmative.

These sympathizers are wholly unable to share the opinions of the exclusionists, and are simply at a loss to comprehend the reason why so much fuss should be made because of a handful of Japanese who compare favorably with European immigrants.

Psychological Nature of the Cause.

The fact that right in the midst of the hotbed of the Japanese exclusion movement there are goodly numbers of unqualified friends of the Japanese suggests that the motives of exclusion as well as inclusion are primarily personal; that is, psychological. We are all human and are prone to pass judgment from personal incidents or experience. A single disagreeable experience with a Japanese may drive a level-headed politician to a frenzy of Japanese exclusion, just as the memory of one Japanese friend may make another individual a consistent advocate of a friendly attitude toward all Japanese. Inevitably limited in the scope of experience, we can only generalize from a few particulars. This is why there are such contradictory attitudes to be found among Californians toward the same problem. In generalizing from particular experience we are more apt to arrive at a conclusion which suits our desires and emotions. We reach our conclusions in ways which

we think promote our interests and please our
feeling. Gain or loss, like or dislike, are two pivots
determining our judgment. Those who think they
gain from the presence of Japanese and those who
like the Japanese, from whatever reason, naturally
tend to welcome them; those who feel the contrary,
incline to advocate their exclusion. At bottom,
therefore, the effort of discrimination arises from
a direct or indirect personal experience with
Japanese which resulted in some sort of an unfavorable impression.

Chinese Agitation Inherited.

With this preliminary we shall see what are the
more obvious factors which give rise to anti-
Japanese sentiment on the Pacific Coast. It is
perhaps beyond doubt, as most authorities insist,
that the Japanese inherited the ill-feeling that early
prevailed against the Chinese, and this for no other
reason than that the Japanese are similar to the
Chinese in many respects and were placed under
the same conditions which caused hostility to the
Chinese. We have already discussed how the
Japanese coolies were used by capital as weapons
to pit against the ascendency of organized labor.
Under the general term "Asiatics" the Japanese
shared at first, and later inherited, the painful experience of the Chinese.

Local Politics.

That the Japanese issue was frequently made the football of minor political games in California is an undeniable truth.   Wholly apart from the consideration of right and wrong, we cite a case of political activity which illustrates such a situation. Writing in the January (1921) issue of the *North American Review*, Mr. R. W. Ryder observes:

All during the late war—while the Japanese fleet was protecting our commerce and other interests by patrolling the Pacific—the most cordial relationship existed between the two peoples.   But the Armistice had hardly been signed before agitation against the Japanese again manifested itself; however, not until it had been resuscitated and energized by one of California's United States Senators who was soon to be a candidate for reëlection.   This Senator, Mr. Phelan, appeared in California early in 1919, and at once made a visit to the Immigration Station at San Francisco and Los Angeles; whereupon he issued a statement characterizing the Japanese situation as a menace.   Next, he addressed the State Legislature on the Japanese question.   Prior to his address, although the Legislature had been in session for almost two months, it had done nothing regarding the Japanese.   But a few days afterward several anti-Japanese measures were introduced. . . .

The particular susceptibility of the Japanese issue to political agitation in California may be attributed to the safety and advantage with which it may be manipulated. The Japanese in California having practically no vote are safe toys for play. The possibility of magnifying the "menace" of the Asiatic "influx" is immensely tempting in this case, rendering it a most effective smoke screen for the tactics of private interests.

The San Francisco *Chronicle* stated, in its editorial on October 22, 1920, under the heading, "It Would Probably Have Been Settled without Trouble but for Politicians," as follows:

Had no attempt been made to drag California's Japanese question into politics we would probably have settled the question satisfactorily and with no fuss. . . .

We think it probable that if the question had not been appropriated by politicians seeking to make capital for themselves it would have been possible to have obtained the coöperation, at least the acquiescence, of the intellectual Japanese leaders in the State, in measures designed to prevent the presence of their countrymen from being or becoming an economic menace to California. . . .

That the question has been brought into politics, where it was not an issue and could not be, that it has been made a cause of irritation between Japan and the United States, and has given Japan a lever to use against us in all matters affecting the Orient, is due to the senior Senator from California, who sought to use the problem to advance his own personal interests.

6

" Yellow Peril."

The imaginary fear of an Asiatic influx, cleverly fermented by agitators, is certainly a strong cause of Japanophobia. Somehow we have a historical fear of foreign invasion. This fear is inculcated and whetted among the Californians by a hideous picture of a Japanese Empire, that, like medieval Mongolia, would send a storming army of invasion. One might gather from the reports of the Hearst papers in California that the Pacific Coast of North America was invaded by a Japanese army on an average of once a month. Whether misled by jingo journalism or aroused by the exaggeration of agitators—whatever the cause—it is simply amazing how large a portion of the California people honestly fear the utterly impossible eventuality of a Japanese invasion.

Quite recently another form of menace was suggested, which, because of its more plausible nature, has been widely circulated. It is the fear based upon conjecture that the Japanese will soon control the entire agricultural industry of California and that they will ere long overwhelm the white population in that State. This apprehension was by far the most effective force in deciding in the affirmative the initiative bill voted on by the California electorate on November 2, 1920.

Propaganda.

Propaganda is autocratic power in a democratic state; it is a subtle attempt at controlling social sentiment by influencing the people's mind through its unconscious entrance. Freud teaches us that each of us is in a sense a complex of boundless wishes. We wish vastly more than our environment offers us; hence, most of our wishes have to be suppressed, thwarted. Now, propaganda appeals to this weakest part of man; it promises us an opportunity to satisfy our arrested wishes. "You are badly off, my friends," a propagandist would say to honest laborers, "because the Japs are here to bid your wages down. We are trying to get rid of them for you, and for this we want your help." A similar appeal can be made with immediate good results to almost all classes of people who have some unsatisfied wish—and all men do have such wishes.

Racial Difference.

It is clearly untenable, however, to argue that the Japanese agitation in California is wholly due to imaginary fear and aversion created in the minds of people by politicians and propagandists. The Japanese themselves are responsible for conditions which often justify some of the accusations, and which prompt exaggeration and misrepresen-

tation.   In the first place, the Japanese are a
wholly different race, with different customs,
manners, sentiment, language, traditions, and—not
of least importance—of different physical appearance.   Were these differences merely in kind, they
would not be very repugnant, but when such
differences involve qualitative difference they are
particularly repulsive.   It is, of course, impossible
to pass judgment upon the relative superiority in
all respects of things Occidental and Oriental; but
western civilization naturally seems incomparably
superior to American eyes.   Mere difference of race
alone gives no unpleasant feeling.   When it is also
a difference of quality, at least in appearance—
and in this all must agree—it arouses our æsthetic
repulsion.

Even if a man be of different race and as ugly as
a Veddah from Ceylon, if he remains a solitary
example, or one of a very limited number of his
kind, he would not only not arouse our antipathy
but would even stimulate our curiosity, and many
of us would spend money to see his quaint customs
and manners.   But when his followers increase in
number and establish themselves in our midst, and
carry on the struggle for existence until they are
in the way of fairly matching ourselves, we begin
to be alarmed and unconsciously learn to hate
them.   This is an exaggerated illustration, but it is

precisely the process which has been taking place in California relative to the Japanese. The fact that the Japanese are looked upon rather favorably in the East is because there they are comparatively few in number and are not competitors of the Americans in the struggle for existence.

Japanese Nationality.

To a certain extent, the anti-Japanese sentiment in California as well as elsewhere is accentuated by the national principles of the Japanese Empire. It has a system of government which for various good reasons is unique. It embraces many points that are considered, from the standpoint of the Anglo-Saxon, undemocratic. The smooth operation of democracy has been hindered by some inherent defect in the national system, by lack of experience in representative government, and by the influence exerted through an unconstitutional power represented by the elder statesmen. To make the situation worse, by means of unscrupulous journalism, the American mind is duly impressed with the assumed bellicose and Prussian character of the Japanese Empire, the hatred of which becomes anti-Japanese sentiment in general.

The Japanese Government, again, adheres to a policy of extreme paternalism with regard to her colonists abroad. It seems true that in case of an aggressive and military government it is from necessity the devotee of a pure race and a solidified population, as Mr. Walter Lippman stated.[1] At any rate, Japan does not wish her subjects to be naturalized nor does she encourage them to lose their racial or national consciousness. This is clearly seen in her policy of dual nationality (which we shall have occasion to discuss later), which aims to retain the descendants of the Japanese who are born in America, and hence are citizens thereof, as subjects also of the Mikado. It is likewise observable in the spirit of Japanese education, which is fundamentally nationalistic, as it was referred to in the second chapter. Such a policy of nationalism inevitably incites the suspicion of countries to which Japanese immigrants go, and discourages the people from making an attempt at assimilating the Japanese. This, together with their nationalistic training and education, renders the assimilation of the Japanese exceedingly difficult.

Modern Nationalism.

What accentuates the difficulty in the situation is that the countries which receive such Japanese immigrants also uphold a policy of nationalism, which runs full tilt against the "influx" of immi-

[1] *Stakes of Diplomacy*, by Walter Lippman, p. 40.

grants who do not readily become amalgamated or assimilated. The inflow of such a population, they claim, threatens and endangers the unity of the nation, and therefore it must be stopped or resisted. This is the capital reason which is being ascribed for the discriminatory effort against the Japanese in California by the leaders of the movement.

Congestion in California.

The Japanese, moreover, manifest a strong tendency to congregate in a locality where they realize a social condition which is a poor hybrid of Japanese and American ways. The tendency to group together is not a phenomenon peculiar to Japanese immigrants alone. Such a tendency is manifested by almost all immigrants in America in different degrees. In the case of the Japanese, however, several additional factors operate to necessitate their huddling together—they are ethnologically different; English is an entirely different language from theirs; their customs are wholly different from those of Americans; their segregation offers advantages and facilities to some Americans who deal with them. The external hostile pressure naturally compresses them into small groups. Whatever the cause, it is true that this habit of collective living among themselves retards the process of assimilation, and, moreover,

makes the Japanese problem loom large in the eyes
of the white population living in adjoining places.

Fear and Envy Incited by Japanese Progress.

In addition to this, a point to be noted is the
increase in number of Japanese and their rapid
economic development within the State of California.   The question of immigration becomes
inextricably mixed up in the minds of the populace
with the problem of the treatment of those who
are already admitted.   They act and react as
causes and effects of the agitation.   The apprehension of a Japanese "influx" expresses itself in
a hostile attitude toward the Japanese already
domiciled there.   Conversely, the conflict arising
from the presence of Japanese in California
naturally prompts opposition against Japanese
immigration.   Now, it so happened that recently,
and especially since the war, the number of Japanese coming to the United States through the
California port has decidedly increased.   This is
due to the increased arrival of travelers, business
men, officials, and students, as a consequence of the
closer relationship between America and Japan,
as we shall see in the next chapter.   Nevertheless,
it incites the fear of the Californians and induces
them to adopt more stringent measures against the
Japanese living in that State.

On the other hand, the economic status of the Japanese in California has been steadily developing. They are entering in some directions into serious competition with the white race. Thus, in agriculture, their steady expansion through industry and thrift has caused alarm among small white farmers. Added to this is the high birth rate among the Japanese, which, because of their racial and cultural distinction, forms a problem touching the fundamental questions of the American commonwealth.

Summary.

By the foregoing analysis of the situation, we see that although the problem of the Japanese in California has been made the subject of political and private exploitation, and thereby rendered unnecessarily complicated and acute, it is, nevertheless, a grave problem which contains germs that are bound to develop many evils unless it is properly solved.

In the following chapters we shall study the status of the Japanese in California in respect to population and birth rate, their agricultural condition, their living and culture, and their economic attainments, with a view to elucidating just wherein lie the precise causes of the difficulties.

CHAPTER VII

FACTS ABOUT THE JAPANESE IN CALIFORNIA— POPULATION AND BIRTH RATE

A KNOWLEDGE of the facts regarding the Japanese population in California is important, because it has been a point of sharp dispute between those who insist on exclusion and those who oppose it, the former arguing that the Japanese are increasing at an amazing rate through immigration, smuggling, and birth, threatening to overwhelm the white population in the State, the latter contending that they are not multiplying in a way menacing to the State of California. The fact that such a dispute prevails in the matter of the number of Japanese suggests that it is, at least, one of the crucial points on which the whole problem rests. This is true in the sense that, if the Japanese in California were decreasing in number as the American Indians are, it would be totally useless to waste energy in an attempt to quicken the final extinction. If, on the other hand, they were to multiply in a progressively higher rate so as to overwhelm the white population, it would certainly be serious both for California and for the United States.

Number of Japanese in California.

This being the case, it is but natural that the enemies of the Japanese should exaggerate the number of Japanese living in California. The leaders of the movement for excluding Japanese estimate their number as no less than one hundred thousand. The report of the State Board of Control of California, prepared for the specific purpose of emphasizing the gravity of the Japanese problem in California, enumerated the population of Japanese in that State at the end of December, 1919, as 87,279. This number turned out to be 13,355 higher than the number reported by the Foreign Office of Japan,[1] which was based on the Consular registrations (including American-born offspring of the Japanese) and the count made by the Japanese Association of America. Most fortunately, the preliminary publication of a part of the United States Census for 1920 removed the uncertainty arising from the discrepancy by stating the exact number of the Japanese in California to be 70,196. The possible cause of the overestimation by the Board of Control is to be found

[1] Report published on October 5, 1920, by the Bureau of Commercial Affairs, Foreign Office, Tokyo, Japan.

in its method of computation. Instead of counting the actual number of residents, it simply added the number of net gain from immigration and the excess in birth over death statistics to the returns of the census of 1910, overlooking the fact that in the meantime a great number of Japanese were leaving California for Japan as well as other States of the Union.

The present number of Japanese is a minor matter compared with its dynamic tendency. The rate of increase of the Japanese population in California in the past may be easily obtained by comparing the returns of the United States Census.

The following table indicates the number and rate of decennial increase:

NUMBER OF JAPANESE IN CALIFORNIA ACCORDING TO THE UNITED STATES CENSUS.

Year.	Number.	Decennial Increase.	Percentage of Decennial Increase.
1880	86	. . . . .	. . . .
1890	1,147	1,061	1,234 %
1900	10,151	9,004	785 %
1910	41,356	31,205	307.3%
1920	70,196	28,840	69.7%

We see from the above table that after half a century of Japanese immigration to the United States, California's net gain amounts to a little over 70,000, the number having increased at an average rate of 14,025 per decade, or 1603 per annum. We also observe that the percentage of decennial increase gradually decreased from 1234 per cent. to 69.7 per cent.

It is useful to compare this development of the Japanese population with that of California in general, because it gives an idea of the relative importance of the Japanese increase. This is shown in the following table, in which the decennial rates of increase between them are compared:

COMPARISON OF POPULATION INCREASE OF CALIFORNIA AND OF JAPANESE IN CALIFORNIA.

Year.	Number.	Decennial Increase.	Rate of Decennial Increase.	Rate of Japanese Decennial Increase.	Percentage of Japanese to the Total Population of California.
1880	864,694	....	.....	....	.0099%
1890	1,213,398	348,704	40.3%	1234 %	.095 %
1900	1,485,053	271,655	22.3%	785 %	.68 %
1910	2,377,549	892,496	60.0%	307.3%	1.73 %
1920	3,426,861	1,049,312	44.1%	69.7%	2.04 %

Thus we see that while the percentage of decennial increase of Japanese has been fast decreasing since the census of 1890, descending from 1234 per cent. to 785 per cent. in the next census, and to 307.3 per cent. in 1910, and 69.7 per cent. in 1920, that of California is headed, on the whole, towards an increase. We also notice that the percentage of the Japanese population to the total population of California also shows a tendency to slow growth, increasing only three tenths of one per cent. during the last decade. As a general conclusion, therefore, we may say that the rate of increase of Japanese in California is slowly declining while that of the total population of California is steadily increasing.

In the next place, how does the status of the Japanese population in California compare with that in the continental United States? In the following table, we compare the rate of increase in California and the United States, and enumerate the percentage of the number of Japanese in California to the total number of Japanese in the United States:

JAPANESE POPULATION IN THE UNITED STATES AND CALIFORNIA.

Census.	Japanese in Continental United States.	Decennial Increase of Japanese in Continental United States.	Rate of Decennial Increase.	Rate of Decennial Increase of Japanese in California.	Percentage of Japanese in California to entire Japanese population of United States.
1880	148	......	....	....	58.1%
1890	2,039	1,891	1,277.7%	1234.0%	56.2%
1900	24,326	22,287	1,093.0%	785.0%	41.7%
1910	72,157	47,831	196.6%	307.3%	57.3%
1920	119,207	47,050	65.2%	69.7%	58.8%

The table indicates that the percentage of Japanese in California to the total number of Japanese in the United States is rather high, justifying the complaint of the Governor of California that during ten years, between 1910 and 1920, "the Japanese population in California *increased* 25,592, but in all of the other States of the United States it *decreased* 10,873. Perhaps, in this last-named fact may be found the reason that makes Oriental immigration a live subject of continued consideration in California."[1]

The truth of this statement, which in other words means that the cause of anti-Japanese agitation in California is due to congestion in that one State, becomes almost indisputable. It is doubly apparent when we consider the reason why the Chinese no longer constitute the objects of exclusion in California while the Japanese do. The Chinese have shown, ever since the launching of the agitation against them in the early '80's, a wise tendency to disperse into other States, thus avoiding conflict with the Californians. The Japanese, on the other hand, appear to cling tenaciously to California, and the more they are maltreated and slandered the more steadfastly they remain in that State. This is apparently due

[1] *California and the Oriental, State Board of Control of California, 1920*, p. 30.

largely to the recognition of the desirability of
California, even with its handicaps, over other
States, but it is also due to their helplessness
to extricate themselves from the situation in
fear of a great financial loss involved in the
change.

The Report of the State Board of Control of
California uses the fact of the decreasing number of
Chinese and the increasing number of Japanese in
California as evidence of the success of the Chinese
Exclusion Act in accomplishing its purpose, and
of the failure of the "Gentlemen's Agreement" in
restricting Japanese immigration.[1]   But, in so
doing, it fails to take into consideration the very
fact which it points out elsewhere, which we have
just quoted; namely, that the number of Japanese
has decreased in all of the other States combined
while it has increased in California. It also fails to
take into account the fact that the number of
Chinese, contrary to the Japanese tendency, has
shown a marked tendency to grow in eastern and
middle western States and to decrease in California.
Thus, for example, the number of Chinese in New
England, the Middle Atlantic, and Eastern and
North Central States increased from 401, 1227,
and 390 respectively in 1880 to 3499, 8189, and
3415, respectively, in 1910, while it decreased in

[1] *California and the Oriental*, p. 27.

the Pacific division from 87,828 to 46,320 in the corresponding period.[1]

The foregoing examination establishes the fact that much of the anti-Japanese agitation in California is due to the congestion of Japanese in that one State, as pointed out by the authorities of California, and as confirmed by the extinction of anti-Chinese sentiment in California, consequent upon the exodus of large numbers of Chinese from that State.

We have seen that the Japanese population in California increased from 86 in 1880 to 70,196 in 1920 at the annual rate of 1403. We shall now see how each of the three factors—lawful entrance of Japanese into the United States, smuggling, and birth—has contributed to this increase.

Immigration.

Without question, the coming of the Japanese who are legally permitted to enter the United States has been the largest factor contributing to their increase in California. Of the total Japanese entering the continental United States since its beginning up to the end of 1920, estimated at 180,000,[2] California claims to have received about two thirds,[3] or approximately 125,000. Since

---

[1] For detailed comparison of geographical distribution of Chinese and Japanese see Appendix I.

[2] See Appendix G.   [3] *California and the Oriental*, p. 31.

7

California's present Japanese population is 70,196, of which about 25,000 [1] are American-born children, it means that out of the total number of Japanese immigrants (125,000) who entered California, only 45,196 survive now in that State, the rest having either migrated to other States, or died out, or returned home.

One reason why the Japanese immigration is viewed with so much apprehension is because the facts of the situation are not rightly understood. The number of Japanese coming to the United States has decidedly increased in recent years, especially since the war, the annual number reaching the ten thousand mark. This would certainly be alarming were it not for the correspondingly large number of Japanese who returned every year. The following table shows the percentage of those who returned out of the total arrivals:

Year.	Arrivals.	Returned.	Percentage of Returned Against Total Arrivals.
1916	9,100	6,922	76%
1917	9,159	6,581	72%
1918	11,143	7,696	69%
1919	11,404	8,328	73%
1920	12,868	11,662	90%

[1] Total number of Japanese born in California so far is approximately 30,000, of which about 5000 have either died or live in Japan.

[2] Annual Report of Commissioner-General of Immigration.

The growing number of Japanese coming into America and the increasing high rate of their return, as shown in the above table, clearly indicate the fact that the character of the Japanese now entering the United States has decidedly changed. The explanation of the high rate of Japanese entrance is to be sought in the growing business, diplomatic, intellectual, and other relations between America and Japan which the recent war brought about. In the field of business, the number of branch offices of Japanese firms employing Japanese clerks and managers rapidly increased in the large cities of the United States. Students who formerly went to Europe for study now flock to America and enter the large universities of this country. Many of the newly rich whom the unique opportunity of the World War has created, have taken it into their heads to see the post-war changes in America and Europe. But these Japanese visitors are not immigrants; they are not coolies; they do not come to America to work and settle. They will give America no trouble, for they stay in this country only a brief period of time. They are America's guests, as it were, and they should not be treated as immigrants. The rough handling of these visitors, as sometimes happens in the Western States, gives them a bad impression of the American people at large.

That most of the Japanese now coming to this country are temporary visitors is shown by the following table which distinguishes non-laborers from laborers:

Year.	Total.	Laborers.	Non-Laborers.	Percentage of Non-Laborers Against All.
1916	9,100	2,956	6,144	67.5%
1917	9,159	2,838	6,321	69 %
1918	11,143	2,604	8,539	77 %

"Gentlemen's Agreement."

It is useful to remember the above fact when discussing the workings of the so-called "Gentlemen's Agreement." It is often alleged that Japan has not been observing the agreement in good faith. Thus Governor Stephens states:

There can be no doubt that it was the intent of our Government by this agreement (the "Gentlemen's Agreement") to prevent the further immigration of Japanese laborers. Unfortunately, however, the hoped-for results have not been attained. Without imputing to the Japanese Government any direct knowledge on the subject, the statistics clearly show a decided increase in Japanese population since the execution of the so-called "Gentlemen's Agreement." Skillful evasions have been resorted to in various manners.

Such an accusation appears plausible when it is examined solely in the light of the high number of annual Japanese arrivals. The accusation, however, falls to the ground when we consider two other facts already pointed out; namely, the correspondingly high and ascending rate of departures, and the increasingly high percentage of non-immigrants against immigrants.

It is provided in the "Gentlemen's Agreement" that "the Japanese Government shall issue passports to the continental United States only to such of its subjects as are non-laborers, or are laborers who in coming to the continent seek to resume a formerly-acquired domicile, to join a parent, wife, or children residing here, or to assume active control of an already possessed interest in a farming enterprise in this country." Accordingly, the classes of laborers entitled to receive passports have come to be designated "former residents," "parents, wives, or children of residents," and "settled agriculturists." Of these, the last item, the "settled agriculturists," has practically no significance, because under that class only four entered America since the conclusion of the agreement. According to the agreement, then, only two classes of immigrants, former residents and the families of residents, are admitted.

This agreement leaves the question of the admittance of non-laborers entirely untouched, permitting the Japanese Government to decide as to who may be classed laborers and who non-laborers. The lack of concrete under-standing between Japan and the United States in this respect is a grave defect in the agree-ment. True, the executive orders issued in connection with the "Gentlemen's Agreement" provide a definition of term "laborer," and state:

For practical administrative purposes, the term "laborer, skilled and unskilled," within the meaning of the executive order of February 24, 1913, shall be taken to refer primarily to persons whose work is essentially physical, or, at least, manual, as farm laborers, street laborers, factory hands, contractors' men, stablemen, freight handlers, stevedores, miners, and the like, and to persons whose work is less physical, but still manual, and who may be highly skilled as carpenters, stone masons, tile setters, painters, black-smiths, mechanics, tailors, printers, and the like; but shall not be taken to refer to persons whose work is neither distinctively manual nor mechanical but rather professional, artistic, mercantile, or clerical—as phar-macists, draftsmen, photographers, designers, sales-men, bookkeepers, stenographers, copyists, and the like.[1]

The weakness of the provision, however, is in the difficulty it gives rise to in practical applica-

[1] *Immigration Laws—Rules of November 15, 1911*, published by U. S. Department of Labor, Bureau of Immigration, March 10, 1913.

cation and in the liability of wrong construction
to be placed by the American public in the administration of the "Gentlemen's Agreement."
The difficulty lies not at all in the lack of mutual
understanding between the American and the
Japanese Governments in respect to this question.
The *modus operandi* arrived at between these two
Governments has worked satisfactorily. But because of the lack of a specified definition of "non-
immigrants" and "immigrants," the distinction
to be made between them, and, consequently,
the granting of passports, as already stated, is
left in a large measure to the discretion of the
authorities of the Foreign Office of the Japanese
Government.

The foregoing defect and the confusion on the
part of the American people suggest that the
adoption of a specific definition of "immigrants"
and "non-immigrants"—in other words, laborers
and non-laborers—on the basis of whether a
person is coming to America for work and settlement or for a temporary visit, seems quite
essential.

The Japanese method of distinguishing non-
immigrants from immigrants, however, has not
been altogether irrational or arbitrary. The established custom is that the Government issues
two kinds of passports, one with a lavender color

design on the front page with the word "non-immigrant" stamped on it, and the other with a green color design with the word "immigrant" printed on the front page. The former is given to those who desire to go to America for business, educational, or traveling purposes, expecting to return home after a brief stay, and who have strong financial assurance. The latter passports, namely, the immigrant's, are given to those who are entitled to enter America, according to the already specified provisions of the "Gentlemen's Agreement," viz. "former residents," "parents, wives, or children of residents," and "settled agriculturists." The passports, however, are not granted even to these classes unless they file a petition to the Government with a certificate from a Japanese Consulate in America certifying the breadwinner in America to be an honest man, with a clean record, who is capable of comfortably supporting a family. In this way, although without a definite standard of regulation, the Japanese Government faithfully adheres to the provisions of the agreement, even to the point of being charged with an extreme rigidity. The following table given in the Report of the Commissioner-General of Immigration shows in detail how the agreement has been operating:

JAPANESE LABORERS ADMITTED TO CONTINENTAL UNITED
STATES 1910 TO 1919.

*According to Annual Report of Commissioner-General of
Immigration.*

Fiscal Year Ending June.	In possession of proper passports. Entitled to passports under "Gentlemen's Agreement."					
	Former Residents.	Parents, Wives, and Children of Residents.	Settled Agriculturists.	Not Entitled to Passports.	Without Proper Passports.	Total.
1910	245	373	1	47	39	705
1911	351	268	..	88	25	732
1912	602	224	..	60	27	913
1913	1,175	178	..	41	13	1,407
1914	1,514	119	..	84	51	1,768
1915	1,545	585	1	54	29	2,214
1916	1,695	1,199	2	39	78	3,013
1917	1,647	1,115	..	36	87	2,885
1918	1,774	507	..	88	235	2,604
1919	1,265	422	..	48	241	1,976
Total....	11,813	4,990	4	585	825	18,217

The table indicates that out of the total immigration of 18,217 from 1909 to 1920, 11,813 of this
number were people who temporarily visited Japan;
4990 belonged to the families of residents; 4 were
"settled agriculturists," and 585 were persons not
entitled, for reasons unexplained, to passports.
It also shows that 825 were persons without proper

passports. The latter category included immigrants bound for Canada, Mexico, and South America who were sidetracked on the way, those who lost their passports, as well as deserting seamen and smugglers. For these cases of illicit endeavors to enter America, the Japanese Government can hardly be held responsible. It would be absurd to put forth the negligible number of 585 cases, that are recorded during the period of ten years as persons who are not entitled to passports, as an evasion of the "Gentlemen's Agreement" on the part of the Tokyo Government. It is one thing to point out the defects of the agreement, but it is an entirely different matter to charge bad faith in its execution.

By way of summary, then, it may be stated that ever since the "Gentlemen's Agreement" was put into effect in 1907, the number of immigrants has gradually decreased, those admitted having been mostly former residents, although the total number of Japanese coming to the United States has increased, due to the growing number of tourists and business men. The agreement, as far as its execution is concerned, has been carried out with the utmost scruple, but it is defective in that it does not clearly distinguish immigrants from non-immigrants, and this leads to confounding visitors with immigrants, and hence to the unfounded claim that it is being ignored, evaded. Judging from the sentiment prevailing in California, and in other Western States, against the Japanese, it is desirable that the agreement be so amended as to forbid the advent of all Japanese, except well-defined non-immigrants and former residents temporarily visiting Japan. This will prevent the further increase through immigration of Japanese settlers in California or elsewhere in the United States. This step is deemed advisable, not that a handful of immigrants as such is serious, but that the main question at issue—the treatment of Japanese already in America—becomes thereby liberated from further complication. It will go far to reduce the fear of Californians, and thereby alleviate the difficulty of the main issue.

Smuggling.

There is no room for doubt that smuggling is responsible for a part of the Japanese population in California. From the nature of the case, it is, however, impossible to estimate the number of Japanese who have entered the United States through this illegal method. During the visit to California last summer, of the House sub-Committee on Immigration and Naturalization for the investigation of Japanese conditions, a rumor was circulated and published in the principal papers of the country to the effect that the Committee had discovered amazing facts as to the systematic smuggling of Japanese into this country through Guaymas. Later, it was made clear that the rumor owed its source to the machinations of certain anti-Japanese agitators who willfully concocted the canard. While it is possible that from the Mexican and Canadian borders a few scores of Japanese may be smuggled in every year, it is absurd to imagine that any wholesale smuggling is being practiced through the connivance of Japanese officials and under the noses of competent officers who patrol the borders and coasts.

It may also be remembered that Japan and Canada have an agreement restricting the number of Japanese entering Canada. This renders the northern borders of the United States comparatively free from the danger of smuggling. Except through desertion of seamen, which numbered 315 cases during the past ten years, it is almost impossible to enter secretly by way of the Pacific Coast. The only danger zone is the Mexican border. But here again there are good reasons for believing that smuggling from Mexico cannot be practiced on a large scale. In the first place, the number of Japanese in Mexico amounts only to 1169,[1] and no passports have been granted by the Japanese

[1] *Japan Year Book*, 1920, p. 34.

Government since 1908 to laborers who wish to go to Mexico.[1] In the second place, the American Government would take care to see that its border-patrol is efficient enough to arrest smugglers. The Mikado's Government, too, has been sincere in co-operating with the American authorities to prevent the evasion of the law.

Birth Rate.

The cardinal question relating to the Japanese population in California is the question of birth rate. Immigration can be restricted, smuggling may be completely prevented, but the fact of the high birth rate is something which cannot be very easily combated without infringing upon traditionally sacred principles and personal freedom. It is quite true that the high birth rate among the Japanese in California would not have been a serious matter if the nationalism of America were as broad as that of Ancient Rome, or if the Japanese were a race which will readily and speedily lose its identity in the great American melting pot. But the fact remains that the United States of America is not merely a mixture of different races and colors; she is a solid, unified, composite country, although she draws race material from all over the world. Nor

[1] *Pacific Review*, vol. i., No. 3, p. 363; "The Japanese in California," by David S. Jordan.

are the Japanese a race likely to amalgamate completely with Americans in a few generations. Thus the question of Japanese birth rate in America becomes a vital matter, touching the fundamental questions of national and racial unity in the United States.

With the importance of the question clearly kept in mind, we shall see what are the facts as to births among the Japanese in California. The following table, prepared from the reports of the California State Board of Health, Bureau of Vital Statistics, shows the number of annual births of Japanese from 1906 to 1919, and its percentage of the total number of births in California:

NUMBER OF BIRTHS.

Year.	Total Births in California.	Japanese Births in California.	Japanese Births— Percentage of Total.
1906	. . . .	134	. . . . . .
1907	. . . .	221	. . . . . .
1908	. . . .	455	. . . . . .
1909	. . . .	682	. . . . . .
1910	32,138	719	2.24%
1911	34,828	995	2.86%
1912	39,330	1,407	3.73%
1913	43,852	2,215	5.05%
1914	46,012	2,874	6.25%
1915	48,075	3,342	6.95%
1916	50,638	3,721	7.35%
1917	52,230	4,108	7.87%
1918	55,922	4,218	7.54%
1919	56,527	4,378	7.75%
Totals	459,552	29,469	

The table indicates in the first place that the birth rate of California as a whole is steadily growing, and in the second place that the birth rate of the Japanese was very low until 1906 or 1907, but since then it has been rapidly growing. The relative percentage of Japanese births in the total births of California, however, indicates the tendency to diminish, having reached the highest mark in 1917, when it was 7.87 per cent., but decreasing slightly in the last few years.

The exceedingly high birth rate of the Japanese in California becomes clearer when considered in terms of the rate of birth per thousand of population. In the year 1919, the number of births in California was 1.79 per thousand population. In Japan, where the birth rate is high, it was 2.53 during the past decade. The birth rate of Japanese in California is more than three times as high as that for the total of California, and more than double that in Japan.

There are several reasons for this abnormally high birth rate among the Japanese in California. In the first place, a large portion of these Japanese are in the prime of life, and moreover they are selected groups of vigorous and healthy individuals. Commenting on the age distribution of Japanese in this country, the report of the Bureau of Census states[1]:

[1] Bulletin 127, 1914, p. 8.

The most noteworthy fact about the age distribution of the Japanese is their remarkable concentration on the age groups 25 to 44, nearly two-thirds of the Japanese being in this period of life. Only 4.5 per cent. of the Japanese are over 45 years of age, as compared with 44.7 per cent. of the Chinese. The explanation is, doubtless, to be found in the fact that the Japanese represent more recent immigration than the Chinese.

The truth of this statement was borne out by the recent investigation conducted by the Japanese Association of San Francisco, which obtained the following result in thirty-six northern counties of California:

AGE DISTRIBUTION OF JAPANESE IN MIDDLE AND NORTHERN
CALIFORNIA, 1920.

Age.	Male.	Female.	Total.	Percentage of Age Group.
Under 7	4,078	3,786	7,864	18.%
8 to 16	2,035	1,663	3,698	8.%
17 to 40	17,037	8,535	25,572	59.%
Above 40	5,683	805	6,488	15.%
Total...	28,833	14,789	43,622	100.

Thus, out of the total number of 43,622 investigated, 25,572 or nearly 59 per cent. are between the ages of seventeen to forty, only 5 per cent. of females being those who passed the age of fertility.

Another reason for the high birth rate of the

Japanese in California is the high percentage of married people. The rate of married people among the Japanese in California suddenly rose since some ten years ago when a great number (between 400 and 900 per annum) of wives began to come in under the popular name, *picture brides*. The ratio maintained between male and female among the Japanese in California was one to six ten years ago, but at present, it is one to two.[1] Since it is estimated that there are 16,195 Japanese wives in California,[2] it is obvious that there are double that number, or 32,390 married Japanese, in California, which means that 46 per cent. of the total population are married. This is apparently a high rate, since it is 17 per cent. in Japan, 36 per cent. in Great Britain, 37 per cent. in Italy. Although exact data is lacking, judging from the fact that only less than a half of California's white population are of ages above twenty-one,[3] it may not be too far-fetched to estimate the percentage of married people at 25 per cent. of the total population.

[1] The following data are reported by the Bureau of Census, Washington, in preliminary publication of 1920 census:

The Japanese population by sex in 1920 is male 44,364, female 25,832; for 1910, male 35,116, female 6,240; and for 1900, male 9,598, female 553. The per cent. distribution by sex of the Japanese in 1920 is male 63.2 per cent., female 36.8 per cent.; for 1910 male 84.9 per cent., female 15.1 per cent.; and for 1900, male 94.6 per cent., female 5.4 per cent.

[2] Gulick, S. L., *Japan and the Gentlemen's Agreement*, 1920, p. 7.

[3] *World Almanac 1921*, p. 476–9.

8

From the foregoing considerations we can deduce this, that the Japanese are mostly at the prime of life, and that the percentage of married people is exceedingly high. Now, in comparing the birth rates of two groups such as those of the Japanese and of the Californians in general, a mere comparison of rates without taking into consideration the difference in age distribution and marital conditions is not only useless, but it is absolutely misleading. California has only 20 per cent. of people between the ages of eighteen to forty-four,[1] while the Japanese group has 59 per cent.; California has about 25 per cent. or less of married population, including those who have passed the fertile period; while the Japanese community has 46 per cent. of married population, all of whom are in the zenith of productivity. No wonder, then, that the Japanese in California have three times as high a birth rate as that of California as a whole.

There is another factor which accounts for the high birth rate of the Japanese. It is the sudden rise of the standard of living. It is an established principle of immigration that when immigrants settle in a new country and attain a much higher standard of living than they were accustomed to at home they tend to multiply very rapidly through

[1] *World Almanac 1920*, p. 487.

high birth rate. Among the European immigrants in this country, a birth rate of fifty per thousand is not rare.[1] In the careful researches made in Rhode Island concerning the fertility of the immigrant population,[2] it was found that their birth rate was invariably high, 72 per cent. of the married women each having upwards of three children, with an average of 4.5 children for each one of them. This fact holds equally good for the Japanese immigrants, most of whom came from the poor quarters of the agricultural communities, where not only economic handicaps but customs and social fetters operate to check their multiplication. When, therefore, they come to California, where food is abundant, work easy, climate salubrious, and personal freedom is incomparably greater, they naturally tend to multiply.

What we May Expect in the Future.

We have seen, then, that the high birth rate among the Japanese settlers in California is due primarily to the facts that the largest portion of them are in the prime of life; that the percentage of married people is remarkably high, the larger part of them, especially the women, being at the

[1] The birth rate of immigration population in Massachusetts was 49.1 in 1910.

[2] *Senate Document*, vol. lxv.; 61st Congress.

zenith of productivity, and that their standard of living suddenly improves when they settle in California. The question naturally arises as to what will be the future development of Japanese nativity. Remembering that a prediction, however scientific, cannot at best be more than a possibility, we shall venture to forecast the future of the Japanese birth rate in California.

In doing so, the proper way would be to examine any possible future change in the causes which constitute the present high birth rate. How, then, about the age distribution of the Japanese? It has been shown that 59 per cent. of them are between the ages of seventeen and forty, and that 15 per cent. of them are above forty. In other words, 74 per cent. of the Japanese are mature, while only 26 per cent. are minors. Now, we are all mortals, and grow old as time passes; even the Japanese do not have magical power to retain perennial juvenility, as some agitators seem to think. They grow old, the Japanese in California, as years come and go, passing gradually into the age when childbearing is no longer possible. Therefore, if fresh immigration is checked, which we have already indicated is desirable, it is manifest that a large portion of the present Japanese in California will die out without being reinforced by youths save those who are born in America, and hence are citizens thereof. That this tendency has already set in may be seen from the increase of the death rate among the Japanese in California, as the following table indicates:

DEATH RATE OF JAPANESE IN CALIFORNIA.

Year.	Number.	Percentage of Death per 1000.
1910	440	10.64%
1911	472	.....
1912	524	.....
1913	613	.....
1914	628	.....
1915	663	.....
1916	739	.....
1917	910	.....
1918	1150	.....
1919	1360	20.00%

The rate of death per one thousand population increased twice during the past ten years.

When the age distribution becomes normal by the passing away of the middle-aged group which constitutes the majority at present, rendering the population evenly distributed among the children, middle-aged, and the old, the present high percentage of married people also will disappear, descending to the normal rate ruling in the ordinary communities, which is but half as high as that now prevailing among the Japanese living in California. When the number of young people relatively lessens, and that of married people also decreases, what other result can we expect but the marked fall in numbers born?

Improved standards of living as a cause of the high birth rate will also cease to operate as new immigrants will no longer enter; and the American-born generations will gradually take their parents' place. The younger generations of Japanese are as a rule higher in culture and ideals than their parents. Accordingly, it is unthinkable, other things being equal, that they should go on multiplying themselves as their parents did. It is an established principle proved conclusively by the thoroughgoing Congressional researches in Rhode Island,[1] that the birth rate among foreign - born immigrants is exceedingly high, and that it steadily decreases in successive generations, reaching the normal American rate within a few generations. We are, then, on a safe ground in inferring that a similar tendency will also manifest itself among the Japanese in the United States.

Our discussions concerning future birth rate, then, seem to point decidedly to the conclusion that since the present high percentage of the middle-age group and the married group is bound to diminish as time passes, and since the fertility of the future generations is not likely to be as high as that of their parents, it will decrease markedly

[1] *Senate Document*, vol. lxv., 61st Congress.

by the time the present generation passes away.
It is, therefore, only a question of time. The
present is a transitional period, a turning-point,
in the history of the Japanese in America. It is
surely unwise, then, to become unduly excited
over the passing phenomenon, and thereby defeat
the working of a natural process which promises
to bring about a satisfactory solution in the not
distant future.

CHAPTER VIII

FACTS ABOUT THE JAPANESE IN CALIFORNIA— FARMERS AND ALIEN LAND LAWS

AGRICULTURE is by far the most important occupation of the Japanese in California. Out of the total Japanese population of 70,196 in California, 38,000 belong to the farming classes including those who are sustained by bread-winners. Besides, there are thousands of laborers who seek farm work during the summer. Perhaps owing to the facts that most of the Japanese immigrants are drawn from the agricultural communities in Japan, that the climate and soil of California are especially suited to the kinds of farming in which the Japanese are skilled—such as garden-trucking and berry-farming—the Japanese in California have been markedly successful in agricultural pursuits.

History of Japanese Agriculture in California.

The history of Japanese farming in California dates back to the time when the Chinese Exclusion Law was enacted in 1882. A number of Japanese laborers were employed in the Vaca Valley and another group in the vineyards of Fresno as early as 1887–1888. Since that time the number of Japanese farm laborers has steadily increased. They have distributed themselves widely in the lower Sacramento, San Joaquin River, Marysville, and Suisun districts. Later many Japanese settled in Southern California. During that early period the Japanese farm laborers were warmly welcomed by the California farmers because of the dearth of farm hands and because of their skill and industry in farming.

But the Japanese were not satisfied at remaining mere farm hands. They saved their wages and attempted to start independent farming. In many cases independent farming was not as profitable as wage labor, since the former involved risk and responsibility. Yet because of the incalculable pleasure which independence brings, because of the ease with which leases could be obtained, and because of the social prestige attached to the "independent farmers," the Japanese developed a distinct tendency to lease or buy land and to take up farming by themselves rather than be employed as wage earners.

This tendency, however, did not manifest itself distinctly until some time later, when they had saved sufficient sums of money to launch such undertakings. Thus the census of 1900 records only 29 farms, covering 4698 acres, which were operated by Japanese. The number steadily increased during the following ten years. According to the census of 1910 they operated 1816 farms, covering 99,254 acres of land. At present it is reported that they own some 600 farms covering 74,769 acres and operate some 6000 farms embracing 383,287 acres under lease or crop contract, bringing the total farm acreage under Japanese control to 458,056 acres.

The brilliant success of the Japanese farmers in California may be better appreciated when the amount and value of the crops turned out by them every year are considered. Governor Stephens, in his letter to Secretary of State Colby, quotes in part the report prepared by the State Board of Control, and states:

. . . At the present time, between 80 and 90 per cent. of most of our vegetable and berry products are those of the Japanese farms. Approximately, 80 per cent. of the tomato crop of the State is produced by Japanese; from 80 to 100 per cent. of the spinach crop; a greater part of our potato and asparagus crops, and so on.

In another part of the letter he remarks:

. . . In productive values—that is to say, in the market value of crops produced by them—our figures show that as against $6,235,856 worth of produce marketed in 1909, the increase has been to $67,145,730, approximately ten-fold.

Causes of Progress.

There are many causes for this rapid development. In the first place, the Japanese as a rule are ambitious. They do not rest satisfied, like the Chinese and the Mexicans, with being employed as farm laborers. They save money or form partnerships with well-to-do friends, and start independent farms. This is made easy by a form of tenancy which prevails in California. That is, the landowner advances the required sum of money to a tenant, offers him tools and shelter, and in return receives rent from the sale of the crops. This is a modified form of crop contract, but it is decidedly more secure for the owner, because he assumes less risk. It is more profitable to the tenant because he gets a due reward for his effort. On account of the ease with which this kind of lease is obtained, ambitious Japanese farm laborers soon become tenants, and when successful —and usually they are—they buy a piece of land with the intention of making a permanent settlement.

That Japanese farmers are usually favorably regarded by landowners is an important factor in their success. Although there have been cases in

which the Japanese provoked the hatred of landowners by not observing promises or failing to
carry out contracts, on the whole, the Japanese are
preferred to other races, because they are more
peaceful, take better care of the land, and pay
higher rent.[1]

The reason why Japanese take better care of the
land and can pay higher rent than ordinary farmers
may be found in their previous agricultural training in Japan.   There the farming is conducted on
the basis of intensive cultivation.   Moreover, in
order to prevent exhaustion of land the farmers are
accustomed to taking minute care that the soil's
fertility be retained.   This habit of intensive cultivation and the minute care of the soil, which are
really inseparable, are maintained by the Japanese
farmers when they undertake agriculture in California.   Furthermore, it so happens that the
climate and soil of California are especially suited
for intensive cultivation.   Such products as vege-
tables and berries, which grow so abundantly in
California, are precisely the kinds of crops which

[1] Of the forty-one answers to the questionnaires sent to the
County Farm Commissioners in California by the Board of
Control asking them to give pertinent facts concerning the
methods used by these races (Orientals) in securing land leases,
twenty-five stated: "The Japanese pay more rent in cash or
shares"; ten said: "Japanese pay ordinary rent" or "use
ordinary means in obtaining lease." *California and the Oriental*,
pp. 56–61.

demand careful and intensive cultivation. The notable success of Japanese farmers in this form of production, therefore, is not an accident. By the introduction of methods of intensive cultivation they have been able to take good care of the land and to pay high rent to the landowners.

That the Japanese are good farmers is attested by the fact that they actually produce more per acre than the other farmers. The Japanese-American Year Book of 1918 has the following comment to make regarding the efficiency of Japanese farmers in California:

In the year 1917 there were 12,000,000 acres of irrigated farm lands in California. From this, California produced crops valued at $500,000,000; that is to say, the value of the product turned out per acre was about $42. Japanese cultivated 390,000 acres and produced $55,000,000 worth of farm products, or $141 per acre. The value of the Japanese farms turned out per acre was, therefore, three and a half times as much as that obtained by California farms in general.

Perhaps the patience and industry with which the Japanese have developed some of the "raw" land of California into productive farm land accounts for their prosperity in such localities as Florin, New Castle, the Sacramento district, and the Imperial Valley.

Japanese Farm Labor.

We may now inquire to what extent the Japanese farmers constitute a menace to the California farmers and to the State of California. In considering this question, it is useful to distinguish between the Japanese farm laborers and the regular farmers.

There are in California at present about fifteen thousand Japanese who are employed in various kinds of agriculture. The number varies according to season. In the summer months it increases considerably, while in the winter it greatly decreases. When the seasonal work is over in a locality, the men seek other jobs in other localities. There is work for them throughout the year, since the climatic conditions of California are such that some crop is raised in some part of the State in almost all months. The agency which adjusts the demand and supply of farm labor is known as a "Japanese Employment Office." There are over three hundred, at least, of such agencies facilitating the supply of labor.

The chief advantage which the employment of Japanese farm laborers offers to employers is, in the first place, their highly transitory character. Most of the Japanese laborers, being men of middle age with no settled homes, go to any place where wages are high. The convenience which the farmers receive from this rapid supply of necessary labor is immense, since the crops handled by the Japanese are perishables demanding immediate harvesting. The transitory facility of Japanese labor is one thing which California farmers cannot easily dispense with and is a thing which the white laborers with families cannot very well substitute.

Another convenience derived from the employment of Japanese farm labor is the "boss system." It is a form of contract labor in which a farmer employs workers on his farm as a united body through its representative or boss. This frees the farmer from the care of overseeing the work, of arranging the wages with the workers, and of taking other troubles. Although this system has given rise to many regrettable complications through the occasional failure of the Japanese to observe their contracts, which leads to the general belief that the Japanese are unreliable and dishonest; nevertheless, this "boss system" remains as the one distinct feature of Japanese farm labor which is welcomed by the California farmers.

There is one more characteristic of the Japanese farm laborers which is unique and extremely important. They are by habit and constitution adapted to the garden farming which prevails in

California. Fruit and berry picking, trimming
and hoeing, transplanting and nursery work, which
require manual dexterity, quick action, and stooping over or squatting, are singularly suited to the
Japanese. No other race, save possibly the
Chinese, can compete with the Japanese in this
sort of field labor. With their training in intensive
cultivation, with physical adaptation to the important agricultural industries of California, and
with the rapid transitory capacity and advantage-
ous system of contract labor, the Japanese farm
laborers constitute an important asset to the
agriculture of California.

There are, however, serious charges made against
this class of Japanese. Perhaps the most pertinent
criticism of them is that they do not observe contracts or promises. This question was very ably
discussed by Professor Millis in his valuable book,
The Japanese Problem in the United States, as
follows:

Much has been heard to the effect that the Japanese
are not honest in contractual relations. . . . So far
as it relates to the business relations of the farmers,
there has been not a little complaint. Much of it,
however, appears to have been due to their inability
to understand all the details of a contract they could
not read. In recent years more care has been taken to
understand all of the conditions of the contract entered into, and the charges of breach of contract have

become much fewer. Another source of misunderstanding has been that some of the Japanese, who think more in personal terms and less in terms of contract than the Americans, have sought to secure a change in their leases when they proved to be bad bargains, and have occasionally left their holdings in order to avoid loss. A third fact is that formerly some undesirable Japanese secured leases. These, however, have gradually fallen out of the class of tenants, so that most of those who remain are efficient and desirable farmers.[1]

Another charge is that they work for lower wages than the white laborers. This may have been true several years ago, but at present it is claimed that the exact reverse is the case. The answers received by the State Board of Control of California to questionnaires sent out by it (one of which was, "Give wage comparisons, with notes on living conditions,") to the County Horticultural Commissioners and County Farm Advisers in the State, agree on one essential; namely, that Japanese farm hands are receiving wages equal to or higher than those paid the white workers.[2]

Mr. Chiba, the managing director of the Japanese Agricultural Association of California, gives the following figures as to wages of Japanese and white farm laborers[3]:

[1] *The Japanese Problem in the United States*, pp. 148–49.
[2] *California and the Oriental*, pp. 56–61.
[3] *Ibid.*, p. 221.

9

	During Harvest.	*After Harvest.*
Japanese common laborers,	$4 per day with meals.	$3.50 per day with meals.
White common laborers,	$3.50 per day with meals.	$3 per day with meals.
White teamsters,	$4 per day with meals.	$3.50 per day with meals.

The charge that the living conditions of Japanese are lower is a thing which cannot be determined by off-hand judgment. Reliable statistics are lacking in this line. In fact, the standard, by which we may safely pronounce our judgment on the question, is not easy to establish scientifically. Food, dress, and dwelling may, on the whole, be taken as the criteria for comparison. The food, however, when it happens to be different in kind between two groups of people, unless the prices are compared, cannot be taken as a sure measure for estimating the higher or lower standard of living. The diet of the Japanese farmer is different in kind from that of the American; but it will be rash to conclude that the Japanese standard of living is thereby lower than that of the American. As a rule, the Japanese feed and dress well. There is perhaps no more liberal spender than a Japanese youth. His weakness lies rather in taking too much delight in making display than in taking to heart the qualities of a miser. In dwellings the Japanese have nothing to compare with the comfortable and durable homes of the Americans. The reason for this deficiency is that the Japanese have no assurance for the future; hence they have no incentive to build permanent homes. At any rate, as long as the Japanese are getting higher wages than the white laborers, and are not underbidding the latter, frugal living and money-saving are wholly a matter of individual freedom, which should not give cause for criticism.

That there are still other shortcomings in Japanese farm laborers must be conceded. They are irascible, unstable, complaining, unsubmissive. These are inborn tendencies of the Japanese, and it is not easy to correct them in a short time.

Concerning the question as to what extent the Orientals displace white labor, the replies given by the County Horticultural Commissioners and the County Farm Advisers of California disclose this interesting fact; namely, that in most counties where Japanese are engaged in farm work they are not displacing white labor, and only in a few counties where fruits are the chief products do they appear to displace white labor to any extent.[1] The truth is that the supply of Japanese farm labor has been diminishing noticeably since the virtual stopping of immigration, while the demand has been on the increase. In 1910, it was reported that

[1] *California and the Oriental*, p. 58.

30,000 Japanese were engaged in farm labor in California[1]; in 1918, there were only 15,794 employed.[2]   Professor Millis observed

The number of Japanese available for employment by white farmers has diminished, and in certain communities to a marked degree.   The total number of such laborers has decreased with restriction on immigration, and the increase in number of Japanese farmers.[3]

Japanese Farmers.

While Japanese farm labor has been diminishing, the responsible farmers have been increasing.   As already stated, in 1909 the Japanese controlled 1816 farms, covering 99,254 acres; but in 1919 they cultivated 6000 farms, embracing 458,056 acres. The value of the annual farm products also jumped from $6,235,856 to $67,145,230 during the ten-year period.   Thus the increase of cultivation area has been approximately four-fold and that of the crop value ten-fold.

For three outstanding reasons the rapid progress of Japanese farmers is envisaged with serious apprehension.   The first reason is found in the words of the Governor of California:

[1] *Immigration Commission Reports*, vol. xxiii., chap. iv.
[2] *Japanese-American Year Book*, 1918, p. 10.
[3] *The Japanese Problem in the United States*, p. 123.

These Japanese, by very reason of their use of economic standards impossible to our white ideals—that is to say, the employment of their wives and their very children in the arduous toil of the soil—are proving crushing competitors to our white rural populations.

This statement, that the Japanese are crushing competitors of California farmers, is in a measure true, but it greatly exaggerates the situation. In California, large farms still predominate, and the average size of a farm is about two hundred acres. The size of the Japanese farm is usually small, the average being about fifty-seven acres. The contrast is due to the difference both in the method of cultivation and in the crops raised by white and Japanese farmers. The crops cultivated exclusively by white farmers are such as corn, fruit, nuts, hay, and grain, which require extensive farming and the employment of machines and elaborate instruments. The Japanese, being accustomed to intensive cultivation, almost monopolize the state production of berries, celery, asparagus, etc., which require much stooping, squatting, and painstaking manual work. Thus there is a clear line of demarkation between white and Japanese farmers based on the difference of training and physical constitution.[1]

[1] For detailed comparison of crops raised by white and Japanese farmers see Appendix E.

It must also be remembered that the crops which are exclusively raised by white farmers are those which constitute the more important products of the State, a greater acreage of land being devoted to each of them. Most of the products which are monopolized by the Japanese are newly introduced kinds, total crop values of which are small, a very limited amount of acreage being used for their cultivation. This being the case, it is clearly misleading to represent the Japanese farmers as "crushing competitors" of all other agriculturists in California. Some of those who follow the Japanese methods of intensive cultivation perhaps find themselves injured by the more efficient and successful Japanese farmers, but the number of such farmers is very small.

That the Japanese work longer hours than the white farmers is true. That they occasionally work on Sundays is also true. The explanation for this is that, being discouraged from taking part in the communal life and activities, they naturally tend to spend more time in work and to seek recreation in work itself. On many of the Japanese farms it is frequently the custom to have a day off during the week instead of on Sunday for the purpose of going to town to shop or to go visiting. It is true that the women and children are often found working in the fields with the men, but this is due to the fact that in intensive cultivation there is much trivial work which children and women can undertake without undue physical exertion. The children are usually allowed to play in the fields around their parents while the parents work, and this is often represented as compelling children of tender age to engage in "arduous toil."

We cannot, of course, ascertain how far the Japanese farmers will in the future push and drive the white farmers out if they are given a free hand; but it is certain that at the present time the sharp competition has not yet commenced on account of the clear division of labor established between the Japanese and white farmers. That the unparalleled success of Japanese farmers should give rise to jealousy and hatred among intolerant American farmers is an inevitable tendency.

The second reason given for apprehension is that the Japanese might soon control the entire agricultural land of California unless preventive measures are promptly adopted. This particular fear was by far the most powerful factor in ushering in and passing the land laws prohibiting either lease or ownership of agricultural land by an Oriental. The groundless nature of the premonition becomes apparent when a few figures are introduced. California has 27,931,444 acres of farm land, of which about half has been improved. The Japanese at the end of 1920 owned 74,769 acres and leased 383,287 acres.[1] It may be true that the lands under Japanese control are usually good lands, but they were not so invariably at the time of purchase. As a matter of fact, most of the lands which Japanese have secured were at first either untillable or of the poorest quality, and only by dint of patient toil have they been converted into productive soil.   Many thrilling stories are told of the hardship and perseverance of Japanese farmers, who have after failure on failure succeeded in their enterprise.   They have indeed reclaimed swamps and rehabilitated many neglected orchards and ranches.   Whatever may be the nature of the land owned by Japanese, however, its amount is truly insignificant.   It forms only 0.27 per cent. of the agricultural lands of California, or one acre for every 374 acres; while the amount leased is 1.40 per cent. or one acre for every 72.8 acres.   This is saying that the Japanese in California, who constitute 2 per cent. of the native population, cultivate under freehold and leasehold 1.67 per cent. of the farm lands of California.   When we recollect that more than half of California's agricultural land—16,000,000 acres—is still left uncultivated, it seems almost preposterous that so much vociferation should be raised because of

[1] Figures taken from *California and the Oriental*, p. 47.

the very limited amount of acreage held by the Japanese.

The weightiest reason offered for the necessity of checking Japanese agricultural progress is the one which almost all leaders of the anti-Japanese movement have emphasized; namely, that the Japanese are unassimilable. If they were an assimilable race, and in the course of a few generations were to blend their racial identity with the American blood, California would have no reason to oppose their progress in agriculture. But they are a distinct people who amalgamate with difficulty, if at all. Were they allowed unhindered development in agriculture, in which their success has been most marked, in the opinion of the exclusionists, they would multiply tremendously in number and correspondingly increase in power to the extent of not only overwhelming the white population of California but also of endangering the harmony and unity of American nationality. This is precisely the line of argument which the Governor of California advanced in his letter to Secretary of State Colby. In its conclusion he states:

I trust that I have clearly presented the California point of view, and that in any correspondence or negotiations with Japan which may ensue as the result of the accompanying report, or any action which the people of the State of California may take thereon, you will understand that it is based entirely on the principle of race self-preservation and the ethnological impossibility of successfully assimilating this constantly increasing flow of Oriental blood.

Accordingly, the question whether or not California is justified in prohibiting the Japanese from the pursuit of agriculture is not to be determined by a consideration of the amount of land they cultivate or the comparative wages they receive, but by the consideration of their assimilability. We shall discuss this pertinent question in the next chapter.

Anti-Alien Land Laws.

The significance of the land issue in itself being slight, as shown by the foregoing study, a casual discussion will suffice on the issue of the anti-alien land laws. The land law of 1913, which was enacted in spite of strong opposition among certain groups of the people of California and on the part of the Federal Government, provided, in summary:

(1) An alien not eligible to citizenship cannot acquire, possess, or transfer real property, unless such is prescribed by the existing treaty between the United States and the country of which he is a subject. This provision takes advantage of the fact that in the Treaty of Commerce and Naviga-

tion concluded in 1911 between America and Japan, no specific mention is made concerning the ownership of farm land. The Treaty provides:

Article I. The subjects or citizens of each of the high contracting parties shall receive, in the territories of the other, the most constant protection and security for their persons and property, and shall enjoy in this respect the same rights and privileges as are or may be granted to native subjects or citizens, on their submitting themselves to the conditions imposed upon the native subjects and citizens.[1]

(2) An alien not eligible to citizenship cannot lease land for agricultural purposes for a term exceeding three years.

(3) Any company or corporation of which a majority of the members are aliens who are ineligible to citizenship, or of which a majority of the issued capital stock is owned by such aliens, shall not own agricultural lands or lease for more than three years.

(4) Any real property acquired in fee in violation of the provisions of this act shall escheat to, and become the property of, the State of California.[2]

This ingenious law was rendered ineffective because the Japanese kept on buying and leasing land in the names of those of their children who are

[1] See Appendix B.
[2] For full texts of land laws 1913 and 1920 see Appendixes C and D.

citizens of this country. Moreover, they resorted to the formation of corporations in which a majority of the stock was owned by American citizens.

The outcome of the situation was the adoption in November of last year of a new land law more carefully framed. The new law naturally aims to correct the defects which led to the evasion of the former law. It is in substance as follows:

(1) All aliens not eligible to citizenship and whose home government has no treaty with the United States providing such right cannot own or lease land;

(2) All such aliens cannot become members or acquire shares of stock in any company, association, or corporation owning agricultural land;

(3) These aliens cannot become guardians of that portion of the estate of a minor which consists of property which they are inhibited by this law from possession or transfer;

(4) Any real property hereafter acquired in fee in violation of the provisions of this act by aliens shall escheat to and become the property of the State of California.

The difference between the old and the new laws is that in the new law evasion is made entirely impossible by prohibiting the Japanese from buying or selling land in the names of their children or through the medium of corporations. A novel feature of the new law is that it forbids the three-year lease which was allowed by the old law.

The opponents of the newly enacted law claim that it is unwise because, if it proves effective, it will have driven a large number of capable and industrious farmers out of agriculture, thereby causing no little inconvenience to the people in getting an abundant supply of table delicacies. Even the report of the State Board of Control admits that "the annual output of agricultural products of Japanese consists of food products practically indispensable to the State's daily supply," and adds that their sudden removal is not wise.[1] If, on the other hand, the law fails— and that there is abundant possibility of it the sponsors of the law themselves admit—critics insist that it will result in no gain, but "it merely persecutes the aliens against whom it is directed, and sows the seed of distrust in their minds," and further it will occasion an unnecessary ill-feeling between America and Japan. Presenting the reasons for opposing the new land measure, the San Francisco Chamber of Commerce stated:

The clause denying the right to lease agricultural lands is ineffective in operation. It may prove irritating to the Japanese people, but it will not prevent them from occupying lands for agricultural purposes

[1] *California and the Oriental*, p. 104.

under cropping contracts for personal services, which cannot be legally prohibited to any class of aliens.

This is what Governor Stephens referred to when he confessed that the law can be evaded by legal subterfuge, which it is not possible for the State to counteract. And California has no lack of lawyers, who are resourceful and ready enough to teach the Japanese the technical way of evading the law.

The advocates of the new law, on the other hand, argued that anything is better than nothing to show their disapproval of Japanese domination in agriculture, and pointed to the Japanese law regarding foreign land ownership as an example of foreigners not being allowed to own land. If Japan does not permit the ownership of land by Americans, they argue, by what right do the Japanese demand the privilege in America? This apparently does not hit the point since in case of Japan the prohibition of land-ownership is not discrimination against any single nation or people, whereas the case of California is. We may, however, cursorily touch here upon the status of foreign land ownership in Japan.

Land Laws of Japan.

Under present regulations there are three ways in which foreigners may hold land in Japan, viz.:

(1) By ordinary lease running for any convenient term and renewable at the will of the lessee. The rent of such leased property is liable to a review by the courts, after a certain number of years, on the application of either party;

(2) A so-called superficies title may be secured in all parts of Japan, save what is called the colonial areas, running for any number of years. Many such titles now current run for 999 years. These titles give as complete control over the surface of the land as a fee-simple title would do.

(3) Foreigners may form joint stock companies and hold land for the purposes indicated by their charters. They are juridical persons, formed under the commercial code of Japan, and are regarded just as truly Japanese legal persons as though composed solely of Japanese. It will thus be seen that in practice foreigners can take possession of land in Japan about as effectually as in fee simple.

On April 13, 1910, the Japanese Diet passed a land law which embodied, among others, the following provisions:

Article I. Foreigners domiciled or resident in Japan and foreign juridical persons registered therein shall enjoy the right of ownership in land, provided always that in the countries to which they belong such right is extended to Japanese subjects, and Japanese juridical persons. . . .

Article II. Foreigners and foreign juridical persons

shall not be capable of enjoying the right of ownership in land in the following districts: First, Hokkaido; second, Formosa; third, Karafuto; fourth, districts necessary for national defense.

Article III.   In case a foreigner or a foreign juridical person owning land ceases to be capable of enjoying the right of ownership in land, the ownership of such land shall accrue to the fiscus [the Imperial Treasury], unless he disposes of it within a period of one year.

Article IV.   The date for putting the present law into force shall be determined by Imperial ordinance.

This law was severely criticized by both liberals and foreigners on account of its too conservative provisions, and as a consequence it was not promulgated by the Emperor for the time being.   In the legislative session of 1919, the Government introduced to the Diet a revised bill embodying more liberal principles and omitting all features in the law of 1910 considered objectionable by foreigners. Unfortunately the Lower House was suddenly dissolved by the deadlock encountered on the issue of universal suffrage before the proposed law was voted on.   The Japanese Government, it is reported, has drafted a new law with the intention of introducing it to the session of the Diet now sitting (January, 1921), the notable feature of which is the inclusion of Korea and other territories among the available lands for ownership by foreigners.

Effect of the Initiative Bill.

Already there are indications that the action of California has had its effect on the neighboring States. Similar legislation is mooted in Texas, Washington, Oregon, and Nebraska. When we consider that in those States the number of Japanese is very small and the amount of land-holding is simply negligible, the only explanation for the proposal is the influence of California, which has been deliberately strengthened by the direct appeal of Governor Stephens to other States for coöperation. In this way California is rather making the local situation worse, for by limiting the scope of discriminatory activity within her doors, she might have found a remedy for relieving the tension found therein through the dispersal of Japanese into other States.

It is not the purpose of this book to enter into a detailed examination of the legal aspects and technicalities of the new land law voted on by the California electorate. It may be found in contravention to the American Constitution by depriving certain residents legally admitted into this country of the "equal protection of the law" as guaranteed by that instrument. The Japanese Government may lay before the Federal Government a formal protest against the land law on the theory that it infringes on the Japanese-American

Treaty of 1911, by running counter to the spirit of
fairness pervading the document in withholding
from Japanese aliens the rights and privileges enjoyed by aliens of other nationalities.   Or it may
be the intention of the Washington and Tokyo
Governments to reach a mutual agreement by
concluding a new treaty which will specifically
state the rights to be conferred upon each other's
subjects, so that subterfuge will no longer be
possible, and, on the other hand, will completely
prevent the entrance of Japanese immigrants.
We are not in a position to gauge the intent and
nature of the proposed treaty, which is understood to be under way between the Japanese
Embassy and the State Department, while it is in
the stage of negotiation or discussion.   Whatever
may be the nature of the *pourparler*, it must be
based on the conviction that neither legal contention nor diplomatic dispute will ever settle the
vexed question.

America is the country of the people, and the
Government is powerless unless it is supported by
the people.   The key to the solution, accordingly,
must be found in the attitude of the people and
not exclusively in legal or diplomatic arrangements.
We are of the opinion, therefore, that the surest
way of removing the difficulty is to study the
causes that constitute the present California un-

rest and endeavor to eliminate them so far as it is within our power to do so. Only by regaining the genuine friendship of the people of California in this way can the Japanese in that State expect to free themselves from the unfortunate unfriendly pressure.

CHAPTER IX

ASSIMILATION

Nationalism and Assimilation.

IN the question of assimilation we find the heart of the Japanese problem in California. The reader will probably recall that, in discussing California's effort to counteract the progress of the Japanese in agriculture, we stated that there would be no ground for justification of the recent rigorous measure except on the assumption that the Japanese are unassimilable, and that they should not, therefore, be allowed to flourish in that State. He will also remember that we stated, in discussing the Japanese population in California, that, were it not for the apprehension of the probable impossibility of assimilating the Japanese, their increase in number either in California or in the United States was not an occasion for anxiety. These arguments implied our belief that the entire problem of the Japanese-California situation would finally resolve itself to one crucial point; namely, the question of assimilation. It is our profound conviction that if it be established that the Jap-

anese are unassimilable, then decisive steps—
much more decisive than any so far adopted—
should be taken by both America and Japan in
order to forestall a possible tragedy in the future.

We hold this view because the present state of
world affairs allows us to entertain no other opinion.
As long as our world order is such that its con-
stituent units are highly organized, composite
nations with independent rights and marked in-
dividualities, it is only natural that each nation
should demand that foreigners entering for the
purpose of permanent settlement conform in a
large measure to the social order and ideals of the
country. In case this is deemed impossible, the
nation opposes any large influx of foreign races because of the necessity of maintaining its national
unity and harmony.

Naturally, this tendency of conserving strict
national integrity is strongest among the oldest
and most highly organized States, and weakest
among the new and loosely integrated countries.
Countries like Japan and England, which have
long, proud histories and traditions, and which are
highly organized, are more strict about the way
they take foreigners into their households. On the
other hand, new countries like Australia and the
South American republics, which have short
histories and few traditions, are more or less liberal

in admitting foreigners. This truth has been exemplified by the history of the United States. She has shown a marked laxity in this regard during the colonial and growing periods; but as soon as she achieved a more perfect national unity and consciousness, she began to manifest a strong tendency toward integration, exerting her energy on the one hand upon consolidation of her population and on the other upon excluding "squatters" who would not readily assimilate.

Whether or not such a nationalistic policy may be considered just, and whatever change the future may witness in this regard, the fact remains that not a single nation in the world at present discards or rejects the policy in practice. In the face of such a situation the only alternative for the Japanese in the United States, when they obstinately cling to their own ways of living and thinking, would be to go elsewhere.

This conviction of ours should not be confused with the hasty, groundless conjecture that the Japanese are a race utterly impossible of assimilation to American ways by nature and constitution. Most of the careless agitators who put forth statements to this effect start from the wrong end in their reasoning. They assume what ought to be proven, and forthwith proceed to formulate a policy on this assumption. They assume that the Japanese are unassimilable and conclude that, therefore, they should not be given an opportunity to progress. This is analogous to saying that because a child is ignorant he should not be sent to school, forgetting that the very ignorance of the child is due to the fact that he has been denied an education. They fail to see that their conclusion is the very cause of their premises. What we maintain is that when the Japanese shall have proved unassimilable, *after all means for their assimilation have been exhausted*, they should then be persuaded to give up the idea of establishing themselves in America.

Meaning of " Assimilation."

A great deal of confusion arises from the ambiguity of the term "assimilation." Its interpretations vary from the idea of a most superficial imitation of dress and manners to that of an uncontrollable process of biological resemblance or identity. Those using the term in the former sense, in face of the fact that the Japanese in their midst dress, talk, and live like Americans, consider it indisputable that they are assimilable. Those who use the word in a narrow sense of ethnological similarity, on the contrary, insist with equal conviction that the assimilation of the Japanese is absolutely impossible. Neither is wrong in reasoning, for assimilation, according to the accepted diction, means the process of bringing to a resemblance, conformity or identity—it is a relative term. Hence, in order to determine whether it is possible for the Japanese to become Americanized, it is necessary to find a standard by which the process can safely be gauged. Without this it is wholly absurd to say either that they are or are not assimilable. If the standard be fixed at physical identity with Americans, the Americanization of the Japanese is hopeless—at least for a few generations; but if it be fixed at conformity with American customs and social order, the Japanese have to a certain degree already been assimilated.

How is the criterion to be determined? Perhaps it may be found, like the standard of our morality, in practical usage; that is, in the accepted usages and customs of the United States. Here we can do no better than point out the traditional spirit of cosmopolitanism, or firm adherence to the policy of racial non-discrimination, which was sustained even at the costliest of sacrifices and which is inscribed in the immortal fourteenth amendment of the Constitution, which states that "All persons born or naturalized in the United States and subject to the jurisdiction thereof are citizens of the United States and of the State wherein they reside."

If the supreme law as well as the traditions and customs of the land do not deny, on account of color or race, any person born in America the right of citizenship, it is apparently un-American to make racial similarity or conformity the standard of assimilability.

A nation, however, cannot maintain its own rights and honor among the family of nations without upholding its individuality. But America's individuality does not consist in ethnological unity alone. It consists more in cultural and spiritual solidarity. America upholds her dignity and national rights with the strength of that patriotism of her people which is born of their active sharing in her culture and ideals, as well as of their common experiences of American life. Clearly, then, one criterion of Americanization is unmixed devotion and allegiance to the cause and welfare of the United States—devotion and allegiance not blindly compelled by force of imposition, but born of voluntary and unrestricted participation in American culture and ideals, religion, and industry; in short, in the entire American life. More concisely expressed, the required standard of assimilation in America is an active share in American life as a whole to such an extent that unmixed love and the will to devote self to the United States are no longer resistible.

The essence of Americanization was elucidated in simple and beautiful words by President Wilson in his memorable speech delivered at Philadelphia in 1915 before an audience of naturalized citizens of that city. He said in part:

. . . This is the only country in the world which experiences this constant and repeated rebirth. Other countries depend upon the multiplication of their own native people. This country is constantly drinking strength out of new sources by the voluntary association with it of great bodies of strong men and forward-looking women out of other lands. And so by the gift of the free will of independent people it is being constantly renewed from generation to generation by the same process by which it was originally created.

You have just taken an oath of allegiance to the United States. Of allegiance to whom? . . . to a great ideal, to a great body of principles, to a great hope of the human race. . . . You cannot dedicate yourself to America unless you become in every respect and with every purpose of your will thorough Americans. You cannot become Americans if you think of yourselves in groups. America does not consist of groups. A man who thinks of himself as belonging to a particular national group in America has not yet become an American. . . .

My urgent advice to you would be, not only always to think first of America, but always, also, to think first of humanity. You do not love humanity if you seek to divide humanity into jealous camps. Humanity can be welded together only by love, by sympathy, by justice, not by jealousy and hatred.

Biological Assimilation.

With this clarified meaning of assimilation or Americanization, let us examine the assimilability of the Japanese. First of all, we shall take up the matter of racial amalgamation. Immediately the questions arise, "Is it possible to amalgamate the Japanese? Is it desirable to do so? Is it necessary to do so?"

To the first question, paradoxical as it may seem, careful observations compel us to reply that it is, and that it is not, possible to amalgamate the Japanese blood with the American. Just as there is no national boundary in science, so there is no human barrier in marriage. Truth and love appear to transcend all natural and artificial obstacles. That love defies racial difference has been amply proven in the United States, where all races are in the process of being fused together. It has no less conclusively been proven by the number of happy marriages that have taken place between Americans and Japanese in this country and in Japan. On the other hand, it is unthinkable that the Japanese should begin wholesale intermarriages with Americans in the near future, to the extent of losing their racial distinction. This is unthinkable because of the social stigma—and Americans as well as Japanese are extremely sensitive on the question of social environment—and the legal and economic handicaps which cause thoughtful persons of both nationalities, who take into consideration the welfare of themselves as well as of their descendants, to refrain from indulging in uncustomary marriages. It is more likely, therefore, that while here and there sporadic cases of intermarriage will continue to take place, and that such cases will gradually increase as the Japanese raise the degree of Americanization, it is wholly out of the question that under the present conditions of social, economic, and political encumbrances, the practice will prevail to any large extent.

This being the case, our second query—"Is intermarriage desirable?"—appears superfluous. Indeed, had it not been for the dangerous dogmatism inculcated by some willful propagandists that the result of intermarriage between Americans and Japanese is "the germ of the mightiest problem that ever faced this State; a problem that will make the black problem in the South look white,"[1] the subject would be purely an academic one. To allow this sort of baseless assertion to go unchallenged is extremely dangerous, because it exaggerates an unimportant point to misrepresent maliciously the whole question of the Japanese in the United States.

[1] Mr. Newman in the hearings held at Sacramento, California, in 1913.

The conclusions of able observers, such as Dr. Gulick and Professor Millis, invariably confirm the fact that, as far as the ordinary means of observation go, the offspring of a Japanese and American couple is in no respect inferior to those of either American or Japanese unmixed descent. Professor Millis states:

So far as experience shows, there is nothing inherently bad in race mixture, if it takes place under normal conditions, and neither race is generally regarded as inferior and the offspring therefore given inferior rank, as in the case of the negro.[1]

From his extensive association with Japanese, Dr. Gulick has been able to make some valuable observations on this topic. He states in his important book, *The American Japanese Problem:*

The offspring of mixed marriages are oftentimes practically indistinguishable from Caucasians. The color distinction is the first to break down. The Japanese hair and eye exert a stronger influence. So far as the observation of the writer goes, there is a tendency to striking beauty in Americo-Japanese. The mental ability, also, of the offspring of Japanese and white marriages is not inferior to that of children of either race.[2]

These observations are valuable in refuting the kind of vile allegations we have quoted. But

[1] Millis' *The Japanese Problem in the United States*, p. 275.
[2] Gulick, S. L., *The American Japanese Problem*, p. 153.

because of the limited number of cases observed, and the necessarily unscientific character of the observation, the utilization of these studies must be confined to pointing out the absurdity of the opposite extreme dogmatism and not extended to the constructive argument.

Even less reliable are the opinions of speculative biologists who by the use of analogy—that is, by examples of hybridization of plants and animals— try to throw light on the subject of racial inter-marriage. In general, the assertions of these biologists agree that the intermixture of races too far apart is undesirable because it results in a breakdown of the inherent characteristics of each, but that the combination of races slightly different is more desirable than intra-racial marriage because it tends to invigorate the stock. To this extent, opinions concur; but as to the question what races may be considered similar and what races different they begin to disagree. Most of them divide the human races by the color of the skin, and state that the case of the black and white races is that of extreme intermixture, and cite that between two white races as a desirable one. When they are pressed to pass a verdict on the result of mixture between the yellow and white races, most of them give only vacillating replies, as in the following extracts:

Yellow-white amalgamation may not be fraught
with the evil consequences in the wake of the yellow-
black and the white-black crosses. At the same time,
it should be pointed out that the Caucasians and the
Mongolians are far apart in descent, and that the
advantages to be gained by either in this breaking up
of superior hereditary complexes developed during an
extended past are not clear.[1]

Professor Castle is more precise in his assertion.
He says:

Mankind consists of a single species; at least no
races exist so distinct that when they are crossed sterile
progeny are produced.

Offspring produced by crossing such races do not
lack in vigor, size, or reproductive capacity. . . .

Racial crosses, if so conducted as not to interfere
with social inheritance, may be expected to produce
on the whole intermediates as regards physical and
psychic characters.[2]

Here, Professor Castle touches on the important
question involved; namely, social inheritance.
Indeed, human civilization is not all that is contained in germplasm. Mankind developed and
accumulated an elaborate system of living conditions which operate independently of biological
processes. However wonderful a brain a child has,
he will have to remain a savage if he is born in a

[1] Jones and East, *Inbreeding and Outbreeding—Their Genetic
and Sociological Significance*, p. 255.

[2] W. E. Castle, *Genetics and Eugenics*, pp. 233-38.

savage tribe of Africa or in a place where the level of culture is extremely low. In discussing the possible effect of intermarriage upon progeny, therefore, the cultural level of parents and their environment must first of all be taken into consideration. It is here that we find ground for opposition to intermarriage between Japanese and Americans at present. With some marked exceptions, the cultural standard attained by the mixed couples has on the whole been not of a very high order. This is inevitable when we consider that intermarriage between Japanese and Americans has not yet received full social sanction, thus obstructing free play to the process of natural selection. Aside from the purely biological consideration, this want of social approval of intermarriage, with its concomitant, an unenviable social position of the parents, results in an undesirable environment for the offspring.

The welfare of their progeny is not the only determining point of intermarriage. Is it, then, sufficiently happy for the couple? Our observations lead us to answer in the negative. To be sure, there are cases of fortunate marriages in which it seems impossible for the couple to be happier. But, on the whole, the husband and the wife often find it difficult to harmonize their sentiments and ideals on account of different antecedents. The inharmony seems to grow as the couple advance in age, rendering their lives miserable. The greatest stumbling block, however, seems to be economic. The Japanese in the United States who are engaged in the ordinary walks of life are offered very little opportunities save in farming on a small scale and in petty businesses. Regardless of their ambition or ability, the Japanese cannot get what are considered in America good positions. Hence, neither their positions nor incomes improve very rapidly— perhaps no advance is made. Most American women are not satisfied to follow a blind alley. They turn back and get a divorce. Exceptional cases, of course, are found in the American-Japanese couples, whose husbands have won distinction and wealth by extraordinary personal ability or by scientific or literary attainments, or by representing great firms of Japan.

Our discussion of intermarriage seems to suggest that it is not likely to occur, for some time at least, in large numbers; that as far as hereditary effect on progeny is concerned, it is wholly premature to pass any judgment at present because of our limited knowledge; but that the social as well as the economic position of the contemporary Japanese in America does not seem conducive to the happiness of either the children of such unions or their parents.

Is Assimilation without Intermarriage Possible?

Let us now consider the third question:—"Is intermarriage necessary for the assimilation of the Japanese?" The people, who argue that the Japanese should be discriminated against because they are biologically unamalgable, thereby commit themselves to maintaining that intermarriage is the only way by which Japanese may become true Americans. Governor Stephens states that California's effort at Japanese exclusion is "based entirely on the principle of race self-preservation and the ethnological impossibility of successfully assimilating this constantly increasing flow of Oriental blood."[1] Without questioning whence he derived the authority for the assertion that the Japanese are ethnologically impossible of assimilation, we wish to refute the contention that the Japanese are unassimilable because they are racially impossible of amalgamation. We believe that racial amalgamation is not a prerequisite of assimilation. We have already shown that the customs and traditions, as well as the supreme law of the United States, do not demand that all Americans be of one and the same race. This fact alone is sufficient condemnation of those baseless utterances which seek an excuse for failure and negligence in successfully fulfilling the duty of

[1] *California and the Oriental*, p. 15.

Americanizing aliens by the camouflage of race difference.

But there are other powerful reasons to support our view that race intermixture is not the only way to Americanize the Japanese. And this we find in the strong influence of environment on the physical and mental make-up of man. Perhaps the most significant anthropological contribution of recent times is the establishment of the truth that race is not a fixed thing, but that it is a changeable thing; changeable according to the conditions of environment. Professor Boas, a recognized authority on anthropology, found, in a strictly scientific investigation concerning the changes in bodily form of immigrants and their descents in America, that aliens change considerably in physical form after they come to America. His conclusions are:

The investigation has shown much more than was anticipated, and the results, so far as worked out, may be summarized as follows:

The head form, which has always been considered as one of the most stable and permanent characteristics of human races, undergoes far-reaching changes due to the transfer of races of Europe to American soil.

The influence of American environment upon the descendants of immigrants increases with the time that the immigrants have lived in this country before the birth of their children.

The differences in type between the American-born descendant of the immigrant and the European-born immigrant develop in early childhood and persist throughout life.

Among the East European Hebrews the American environment, even in the congested parts of the city, has brought about a general more favorable development of the race, which is expressed in the increased height of body (stature) and the weight of the children.

There are not only decided changes in the rate of development of immigrants, but there is also a far-reaching change in the type—a change which cannot be ascribed to selection or mixture, but which can only be explained as due directly to the influence of environment. We are, therefore, compelled to draw the conclusion that if these traits change under the influence of environment, presumably *none of the characteristics of the human types that come to America remain stable.*[1]

A very similar result has been reached by Dr. Fishberg in his study[2] of the Jews in America, in which he found that the physical features of the Jews in the United States are changing considerably as the result of change in social elements.

Because of lack of scientifically established data pertaining to the physical change of Japanese descendants in America, we forbear from making

[1] "Changes in Bodily Form of Descendants of Immigrants." *Senate Document No. 208*, pp. 7-54.
[2] *The Jews: A Study of Race and Environment.*

any bold assertion on that topic. Yet, even to the casual observer, it seems almost undeniable that American-born Japanese children are fast departing from the type which their parents represent, thus corroborating the truth discovered by scientists. The Japanese Educational Association of San Francisco once conducted an extensive physical examination of Japanese children in twenty different grammar schools in California, and found (1) that they are generally superior in physical development to children of corresponding ages in Japan; (2) that in height they are from one to two inches taller than children in Nippon; (3) that in weight they are from three to seven pounds heavier; (4) that they have fairer skin when compared with that of their parents born in Japan; (5) that their hair is dark brown and not jet black, as is that of their parents; and (6) that their general posture is much better than that commonly seen among the children of Japan.[1]

These purely bodily changes of American-born descents may be attributed to the difference in diet, in mode of living, in climate, and in the mysterious power of the social *milieu*, of whose influence upon the physiology of man we are yet uninformed. It is well to remember that America is a wonderful melting pot which does not depend,

[1] See Appendix A.

in its functions, solely upon the biological process of cross-breeding, but also in a good measure upon the social and natural process of automatic conformity to type.

Cultural Assimilation.

The real criteria of Americanization being, as we have seen, a genuine patriotism and cultural refinement, it is in the light of these two points, more than in any other regard, that the question of Japanese assimilability must be examined. Patriotism is a peculiar emotion manifesting itself in love of one's own country, in willingness to devote one's self for the maintenance of national honor and welfare. It arises in us from our association, since early childhood, with things that surround us. We love things that we are used to; we cherish the mountains, rivers, and trees among which we were brought up; we hold dear the friends and people with whom we associated in our early childhood, and as we grow mature, we take pride in finding ourselves members not only of local communities and societies of various sorts but also of the family of a great nation whose ideals and history we inherit. These and numerous other things become a part of our life for which we do not hesitate to fight, and if necessary to lay down our lives.

This suggests that two things are necessary for the genesis of patriotism—native birth and a free sharing in the goods of life. While no generalization can be made off-hand, introspection reveals that, when we migrate to another country after we have grown up, it seems well-nigh impossible to find ourselves emotionally attached as closely to the adopted country as to the country of our birth. To *be born* in a country is the strongest factor in one's patriotism. The Constitution of the United States in claiming all persons born in America as its citizens is clearly a product of master minds. Nativity alone, however, is not often sufficient to enkindle the fire of patriotism in our hearts. In the slave, to whom most of the goods of life were denied, to whom no active share in communal life was allowed, who was treated not as a member of the nation but as a tool, could mere nativity arouse strong love for his country? Only when the child is brought up in an environment of friendly spirit, encouragement, and sympathy does he learn to identify himself with the country.

How do we find the patriotism of the Japanese in America? Are they patriotic in relation to the United States? For all those Japanese who came to America as immigrants of mature age with the prime object of making money, the answer must be made in the negative. Born and reared in the beautiful country of Nippon among a most hospitable people, their love of Japan is surely stronger than their love of America. Trained and educated in the customs and traditions of Japan, imbued with the belief, ideas, and ideals that are peculiar to Japan, they would not know even how to avail themselves of the opportunity, supposing they were granted the rights and the freedom to share in the now forbidden privileges. To complete the inhibition, there are all sorts of handicaps placed on them, making it unthinkable that they should love this country. They cannot vote, they cannot get public positions, and now they can neither own nor lease the land in California. No; the Japanese immigrants in America do not love America more than they love Japan.

Assimilability of Japanese Immigrants.

How, then, about their cultural conditions? It is impossible here to compare the culture of the Japanese *en masse* with that of other people. We can take only a few specific points and see how they stand. Of course, in the absence of accurate data our conclusions are necessarily unscientific.

It is often alleged that the Japanese in the United States have a different standard of morality from that of the Americans, and as evidence of this allegation the attitude of Japanese men towards women is pointed out. Japanese men are really "bossy" in their attitude toward women, but that is the outcome of custom and should not be charged against their morals. They are often accused of being tricky, untrustworthy. We have already seen that there have been cases that justify such accusations, but that the cause was mostly due to their ignorance of legal processes and obligations, in which they sadly lack training. On the whole, the Japanese in America are law-abiding; they very rarely become public charges, and are peaceful and industrious. These facts even the most uncompromising Japanese exclusionist, Mr. J. M. Inman, admits as true, and states further that they are "sober, industrious, peaceful, and law-abiding, and contain within their population neither anarchists, bomb-throwers, Reds, nor I. W. W.'s."[1]

That the Japanese in America have been able to make rapid progress in the Christian religion has been due to the generous aid and wise direction of the American churches. Within less than thirty years Christianity has become deeply rooted among the Japanese communities, exerting the most wholesome and powerful influence in uplifting their living conditions. In 1911, the *Den Do Dan*, or Japanese Inter-Denominational Mis-

[1] *The Forum*, January, 1921, p. 3.

sion Board, was organized with a view to carrying on a systematic campaign for evangelistic as well as community service. The Mission Board has been successful in propagating Christianity among the Japanese. This is clearly shown by the fact that at the present time there are sixty-one Protestant churches on the Pacific Coast, besides fifty-seven Sunday schools. The greatest success of the Board, however, has been attained in the field of practical social service, where the organization of young people's Christian associations, the campaign against gambling and other vices, relief work among the needy, and the promotion of Americanization, have been successfully carried out.[1]

Judging from the small percentage of illiteracy and the complete system of Japanese compulsory education, the Japanese in America do not seem to be much behind the corresponding elements in the American population in average intelligence. Only in English are they markedly weak. The importance of a knowledge of the language in assimilation can hardly be exaggerated. It is the gate through which the alien can arrive at an understanding of American institutions and culture. The weakness of the Japanese in English is chiefly

[1] For this as well as other information the authors are indebted to Mr. S. Kusama, who furnished us with the materials which were carefully prepared by him from first-hand research in California.

due to the radical difference of the language from
their own. Statistics indicate, however, a decided
increase in the number of those who can command
English. The census of 1900 showed that less than
40 per cent. of the Japanese in America could
speak English, but in the census of 1910 the rate
increased to 61 per cent.[1] The rate for foreign-
born whites in 1910 was 77 per cent.

The economic status of the Japanese appears to
be about the same as that of European immigrants.
This is indisputable from the sheer fact that the
earnings of both are about the same. The only
difference is that the Japanese show a tendency to
mediocrity of earning power without becoming
either paupers or millionaires. This is due to the
fact that while there is an abundance of work
offered to Japanese which enables them to earn a
comfortable living, all avenues for a greater economic success are closed to them. No sooner do the
Japanese show signs of some small success in agriculture than the privilege to till the soil is denied
them. A similar restraint is now being attempted
on the Japanese progress in fishing in California.
In a sense, economic welfare is the foundation of
cultural and spiritual progress, and to be denied
the opportunity to make progress in this field is a
heavy disadvantage.

[1] *Bureau of Census Bulletin 127*, p. 12.

The gravest defect of the Japanese is their lack of training in democratic institutions. Having been given little opportunity to share in public or political activities in Japan, their understanding and training in civic duties is notoriously weak. Obviously this must hinder the process of Americanization to a great extent. To counteract this weakness the dissemination among them of a knowledge of American civics is necessary. It may be most effectively done by allowing them to share in a measure the American communal activities. But this is a privilege denied them.

The foregoing discussion of the cultural conditions of the Japanese in America is important, not in determining whether or not the Japanese immigrants are qualified to become American citizens— for this is out of the question at present, since the right of naturalization is not granted to them— but to show what is the character of the influence which is exerted upon the native-born Japanese, Americans by birth, by their parents. The core of the Japanese problem in America is, in our opinion, whether or not American citizens of Japanese descent can become worthy Americans. Those immigrants who came from Japan will die out in the course of time, and further immigration can be stopped. In this way it is possible to curtail to a minimum the number of alien Japanese in the

United States. But the American-born Japanese
are American citizens and they are here to stay.
Whether these young Americans will become a
strong and successful element of the American
people or whether they will degenerate to a kind
of parasite and become America's "thorns in the
flesh" is really a question of cardinal importance.
But this depends much on the freedom and opportunity which are extended to their parents in this
country. Thus the treatment of the Japanese in
California or elsewhere in the United States assumes an aspect of vital significance to the nation.
It is not a question of the abstract principles of
justice or equality alone, but one of concrete and
vital interest to America's own welfare.

It is in this connection that all sorts of pressure
and oppression—economic, political, social, and
spiritual—exerted on the Japanese population,
become most objectionable and harmful. These
discriminatory efforts against the Japanese obstruct the Americanization of native-born Japanese
in two ways. They prevent the parents from becoming well-to-do and refined people, and from
getting permanent occupation and homes, all of
which are essential if parents are to bring up their
sons and daughters to a respectable standard.
They also unconsciously imprint on the tender
minds of children the idea that their fathers and

mothers were not treated kindly in America, whose
loyal citizens they are destined to become. What
do those exclusionists really mean, when they insist that the Japanese should be given no opportunity to progress either in agriculture or industry
because they are unassimilable people? Do they
mean thereby to check Japanese immigration?
They surely cannot mean this, for there are other
and more friendly ways of achieving their object,
since Japan has more than once expressed her
willingness to coöperate with America in this
respect. What else can they mean but that they
want to hinder the American citizens of Japanese
descent from becoming worthy Americans by
ostracizing and persecuting their parents?

Native-Born Japanese.

Fortunately, in spite of all unfavorable influence
and environment created for them, the native-
born Japanese show very hopeful signs of realizing
perfect Americanization. Here again we do not
wish to dogmatize, in apparent lack of scientific
data, and assert that we need feel no apprehension. Yet the few data gathered on the subject
from observation strongly point to the hopeful
conclusion that as greater numbers of them approach mature age they are gradually becoming
Americans by the accepted standard. They

proved their patriotism to America during the great war by enlisting in the American army and navy. In their manner, address, and temperament these boys and girls are American, with an unconcealed air of American mannerism. In their fluent and natural English, in their frankness and bold recklessness, in their dislike of little and irksome tasks and love of big and adventurous undertakings, in their chivalry and gallantry, in their tall and well-built stature, these young people are wholly American, no longer recognizable as Japanese except in their physical features. Indeed, it is the common testimony of the Japanese visiting America that the Japanese children born and reared here differ so distinctly from children in Japan that in their manners, spirit, and even in the play of expression on their faces, they appear characteristically American. We cannot help being surprised by the completeness with which the so-called racial traits of the Japanese are swept away in the first generation of Japanese born in America.

The explanation for such a remarkable fact must be sought in the strong influence of social, national, and spiritual environment. We have seen how even the most stable elements of man's physiological constitution may change in a new environment. This being the case, it may not be entirely surprising that less stable elements, such as temperament and expression, should change more rapidly and completely in a new social *milieu*. This fact is a deathblow to the theorists who uphold the *à priori* view of race, that it is a fixed, pure, unchangeable reality. It attests the truth of Mr. John Oakesmith's thesis in which he so ably establishes that "the objective influence of race in the evolution of nationality is fiction," and that the sole foundation and unifying force of nationality is the "organic continuity of common interest." [1]

In the cross-examination of native-born Japanese children by the Congressional Sub-Committee on Immigration and Naturalization conducted on the Pacific Coast last spring, it was found that in almost all cases the children expressed the feeling that they like the United States better than Japan because they are more familiar and closely associated with things and people in America. This is doubtless an honest confession of their sentiment. They generally do not read or write Japanese because it is wholly different from English and so difficult. They learn from their parents that the life is hard and competition is keen in Japan. They know America is a great country, a land of liberty and opportunity. Naturally

[1] *Race and Nationality*, Frederick A. Stokes Co., New York, 1919.

their interest in Japan is very slight, and they think they are Americans, and they are proud of it.[1]

These are the hopeful signs which offer us reason for being optimistic. We cannot, nevertheless, be blind to the fact that there are many obstacles which if left unchecked will tend to defeat our hopes. These obstacles we find, first, in the congested condition of the Japanese on the Pacific Coast. For convenience and benefit the Japanese have been living more or less in groups, speaking their own language to a large extent, and retaining many of the Japanese customs and manners. This tendency has been a great obstacle in the assimilation of the Japanese. Their dispersal in many other States of the Union is one of the first requirements of Americanization, and consequently of an equitable solution of the Japanese-California problem. We shall touch upon this subject in the concluding chapter.

[1] See example of testimony in Appendix L.

See also Appendix M in which the subject of comparative standing of intelligence and behaviour of native-born Japanese children and American children is discussed by several principals of elementary schools in Southern California.

CHAPTER X

GENERAL CONCLUSION

IN dealing with the Japanese problem in California, we started with a general account of Japanese traits and ideas. We did so because we believed that a knowledge of the Japanese disposition is essential to a comprehensive understanding of the problem. No attempt was made to determine whether the traits of the Japanese—their emotional nature, their well-developed æsthetic temperament and strong group consciousness, and the unique feature of chivalry and virility prevailing among the lower classes—are inherent in the race or acquired; but we concluded that the question may best be answered by observing those of Japanese descent born and reared in different countries. Later, when we examined the characteristics of the American-born Japanese and discovered that they appear to have lost most of the Japanese traits, and, in turn, have acquired mental attitudes that are peculiar to the American, it was suggested that none of the racial characteristics is necessarily fixed, and that, similarly, the Japanese traits must have been largely acquired through peculiar natural surroundings and social systems.

Next we reviewed in a brief way Japan's Asiatic policy in order to envisage the international situation in which she finds herself and to see how she proposes to meet her difficulties at home and abroad. We commented on the manifest shortcomings of that policy. In view of the fact that Japan's industry—her only hope in the future—has to depend largely on the supply of raw material from her Asiatic neighbors, the assurance of goodwill and friendly coöperation with them is essential for her welfare. It is in the failure to obtain this assurance that the defect of Japan's past Asiatic policy becomes apparent. We expressed our conviction that under the circumstances the best that Japan can do is to so reconstruct the principle of the policy as to convince her neighbors of her genuine sincerity.

In the chapter on the background of Japanese emigration, an attempt has been made to discover its causes. The principal causes found are the small amount of land, the dense population, and the limited prospect of industrial development due to the scarcity of raw material. Moreover, the peculiar social and political conditions in Japan are such as to obstruct, by numerous fetters and restraints, the free development of ambitious

youths. The exaggerated stories of great opportunities in the new worlds kindle the desire of the
young people to go abroad.

Tentative attempts were made some thirty
years ago in emigration to Australia, Canada, and
the United States. Nearly a quarter of a century's
effort at emigration into the new worlds, with the
exception of partial success in Brazil, had proved a
complete failure, and thus attempts at migration
towards the North came into vogue.

In our discussion of the causes of anti-Japanese
agitation in California, it was made clear that the
explanation of much of the trouble lies in the
conditions of the Japanese themselves, such as
congestion in particular localities and different
manners and customs. The nationalistic policy
of Japan was also pointed out as a factor making
for resentment. What renders the situation unnecessarily complicated, leading to a general misunderstanding, is the employment of the issue in
local politics—exploitation of the subject for private ends by agitators and propagandists.

Then our study entered the heart of the California problem, the fact of the existing Japanese
population. It was discovered that the rate of
increase of Japanese population in California has
been rapid, but that it shows a tendency to slow
down, while the rate of increase of the entire popu-

lation of the State shows a tendency to steady increase. We found that in comparison with the total number of Japanese in the United States the percentage of Japanese in California is remarkably high, nearly 60 per cent. of them being domiciled in that one State. Then we examined the factors—immigration, smuggling, and births— which contributed to the increase of the Japanese population in California. Under the subject of immigration it was made clear that the net gain from immigration has become small since the restrictive agreement was concluded, but that the number of those entering the country increased because the number of those who are passing through or temporarily visiting America has increased. We expressed our opinion that in order to quiet the excitement of the people of the Pacific Coast it is entirely desirable to stop sending Japanese immigrants to America.

We have somewhat fully treated the subject of birth because it is a vital part of the question. It was discovered in the discussion that the birth rate of the Japanese in California is exceptionally high, due to the fact that a high percentage of the immigrants are in the prime of life and that the percentage of married people is remarkably high. In forecasting the future of the birth rate we stated that if immigration is stopped the present

generation will in time pass out without being re-
enforced, leaving behind American-born children,
who, with higher culture and more even distribution with regard to age and marriage, will not
multiply at nearly so high a rate as their parents.
We concluded, therefore, that the present is a transitional period and that apprehension over the
high birth rate is entirely unwarranted.

The chapter on Japanese agriculture in California gives report of a degree of progress that has
been remarkable. As to the causes of this progress
the peculiar adaptation of the Japanese farmers to
the agricultural conditions of California was presented as the principal one. Then we considered
separately the Japanese farm labor and the farmers.
What we found in treating the subject of Japanese
farm laborers was that they are indispensable to
California's agriculture, inasmuch as they have
several important peculiarities which are useful.
Their ability to farm and their aptitude for bodily
and manual dexterity, as well as their highly
transitory character under the system of contract
labor, are useful assets to the farmers of California.
Under the topic of the Japanese farmer, we examined the reasons given for the discrimination
against Japanese in agricultural pursuits. The
first reason—that they are "crushing competitors
of California farmers"—was criticized on the

ground that there is not much competition between white and Japanese farmers, since there is a
pretty clear line of demarkation between them, the
former being engaged in farming on a large scale
and the latter engaged in small intensive agriculture. The second apprehension—that the Japanese farmer, if left unchecked, will soon control
the greater part of California agriculture—was
characterized as an entirely exaggerated fear, since
the portion of land which the Japanese till is
quite negligible and there are vast tracts of land
yet uncultivated. The third objection—which
finds reason for opposition in the unassimilability
of the Japanese—we held as the weightiest count,
and withheld criticism until we had fully treated
the subject of assimilation in the succeeding chapter. What we insisted on was that it is unwise to
maltreat the Japanese on the surmise that they are
unassimilable. Whether they are assimilable or
not—and this is not the question, for they are not
allowed to become American citizens—their children, who are Americans by virtue of birth, will suffer much from a hostile policy towards their parents.

The anti-alien land laws were considered briefly,
and the views of their critics were introduced.
As an effective measure to cope with the legislation, we suggested that neither legal nor diplomatic disputes will bring about a satisfactory

result, but that only through obtaining the good-will and friendship of the people of California can there be a true solution.

The topic of assimilation discussed in the preceding chapter needs no recapitulation.

The foregoing study, which we have undertaken from the outset with an open mind and fair attitude, has, it is to be hoped, disclosed that the underlying cause of the entire difficulty is a conflict or maladjustment of interest.   There are four parties whose peculiar interests and rights are seriously involved in the situation.   First and foremost, we have to consider the rights and interests of California.   Then we have the United States, which is no less directly concerned with the problem.   For the Japanese living in California, the issue is a matter of life and death; their entire interests and welfare are at stake.   Japan also is as much concerned with the fate of her subjects in America as the United States would be with the welfare of her people living abroad—say in Mexico. The Japanese problem in California is the concrete expression of the maladjustment of the interests and rights of these four parties concerned.

Various measures, wise and unwise, have been proposed for the solution of the problem, but none of them has so far been put into effect, since each has failed to adjust the interests and rights of all parties concerned in an harmonious way, and hence has met with violent protest at the outset.

Take, for instance, the proposal that the Japanese should be granted the right of naturalization. The promoters of the project insist that the denial to the Japanese of the right to become citizens of the United States is the cause of the anti-Japanese exclusion movement, and, accordingly, that the granting of the privilege will annul all discriminatory efforts. Undoubtedly the proposal was well meant, but it has perhaps done more harm than good. In the first place, it confuses the cause and method of discrimination against the Japanese. The Japanese ineligibility to citizenship has certainly been seized on as a weapon for discrimination, but it is by no means the cause. The cause is elsewhere. In the second place, the advocates of the proposal argue that, if adopted, it will defeat the entire discriminatory efforts of the Californians. It is, however, decidedly unwise to attempt to defeat the effort without removing the cause of the difficulty. No wonder the proposal has provoked the wild criticism of California leaders. The granting of citizenship to refined and Americanized Japanese is in itself a proper and desirable step, but to use it as a weapon to defeat the exclusion movement is clearly unwise.

The solution of the Japanese problem in California, if it be equitable at all and satisfactory to the four parties involved, must rest on the following basic principles:

1. *That it should be in consonance with justice and international courtesy; it must redress Japan's grievances and meet America's wishes.*

2. *That it should be fair to Californians; that is to say, operate to allay the fear they entertain of the alarming increase of Japanese in numbers and economic importance.*

3. *That it should be fair to the Japanese residents, both aliens and American-born, so that they may enjoy in peace, without molestation or persecution, the blessings of "life, liberty, and the pursuit of happiness," and participate, as all American-born are entitled and in duty bound to do, in the promotion of the State's well-being.*

The new treaty, which is reported to have been laid for final decision before the Washington and Tokyo Governments by the two negotiators, Ambassador Morris and Ambassador Shidehara, has not been made public at this writing. We have, therefore, no means of knowing the contents or nature of its provisions. It may, however, be presumed that it will go a long way toward redressing Japan's grievances and meeting America's wishes. The latter will probably be met by Japan's

adoption of drastic measures to check completely
the influx of her immigrants. Knowing that Japan
has always been sincere and ready to yield to the
wishes of the United States, we hold it only just
that she be saved the embarrassment arising from
discrimination against her subjects in America.
Proud and sensitive, Japan takes to heart the
abuses or indignities which she deems seriously
detrimental to her national honor.

The conclusion of the Treaty and its ratification
by the Senate, however, may not prove the pana-
cea for all evils, for governmental action is naturally circumscribed in its sphere. To solve the
perplexing question once for all, the Treaty must
be supplemented by the patriotic efforts of public-
spirited citizens of both countries to heal and adjust
the irritated parts in the scheme of American-
Japanese relations which are beyond the reach of
governmental action. Viscount Shibusawa and
some of his compatriots have, during the last year,
held many conferences with some prominent
Americans—those representing the Chamber of
Commerce of San Francisco and the party headed
by Mr. Frank Vanderlip. A better understanding
of the situation must have resulted as a consequence of the conferences. The earnestness of the
Viscount and his friends to do what they could for
the good of both countries is beyond praise. But

we fear they have been measuring America by Japan's standard and trying to cure the trouble without remedying the cause. In Japan the counsel of a few influential men often proves effective even in local affairs, but in America, where local autonomy is strongly entrenched, a man, however prominent a figure he may have cut in national affairs, will think twice before he pronounces judgment on matters of local concern, lest it be construed as an intrusion, and thus defeat the good intention. The California question can only be settled by or in coöperation with the Californians, and right on the spot, not elsewhere.

We believe that the time has come, therefore, when those public-spirited citizens of both countries should replace academic discussion by action. As a means of alleviating the situation we venture to offer the following modest suggestion:

1. That a Committee of a dozen or so members, consisting of public-spirited men of broad vision of both countries, and particularly of California, be formed with the object of formulating and putting into effect the project of relieving the congestion of Japanese in California.

Such a Committee would doubtless be able to secure the hearty coöperation of The Japan Society of New York and other cities, as well as of the Japanese Association of America and similar organizations, all of which exist with a view to promoting friendly relations between America and Japan.

2. That the said Committee appoint an administrator of proved executive ability and a staff for the prosecution of the project.

3. That to finance the project an initial fund of half a million dollars be raised by contribution from the 120,000 Japanese living in this country.

The Japanese domiciled in this country have the keenest interest in the subject; they are directly or indirectly affected by the anti-Japanese agitation in California; they would not grudge a contribution of a small sum for the purpose of uprooting the cause of that annoyance. The Japanese in California who have interests at stake would surely be more than willing to contribute their quota to the fund. The native Californians, too, we strongly feel, in their calm and considerate mood, would obey the dictates of wisdom to adopt a more liberal and logical method of relieving the local tension than to resort, as at present, to measures of repression and persecution.

We are of the opinion that there would be a fair demand in other States of the Union for such skilled farm hands as we have found in the Japanese in California if the facts were well advertised. If proper precaution be taken so as to avoid the repetition of the same story of congestion as that in California, the plan of dispersal above outlined might prove a boon to all concerned.   If the initial stage of the plan be earnestly carried out before the eyes of the Californians, a totally different atmosphere might be created among them so as to win their good will and enlist their coöperation. When such a happy outcome is obtained, a solution of the Japanese-California problem is assured.

There is certainly a great deal which the Japanese in California can and must do.   In the first place, they must thoroughly grasp the psychology of the Californians.   They must indicate, if they are to remain in this country, their willingness to become Americans regardless of barriers or opposition.   They must show this willingness not only in intention but also in practice.   They must improve their command of English, alter many of their customs and manners.   They must endeavor to elevate their standard of living and culture.   They must give up beliefs and ideals which are Japanese and which run counter to the American.   It would be well for them to refrain from building in California Shinto shrines and Buddhist temples and from maintaining language schools.   They must above all learn to take an interest in the national life of the United States.

There is also much that the Japanese Government can do. Its policy of paternalism, extending too much care to Japanese domiciled abroad, and even to Japanese born abroad, must, in our opinion, be altered. The claim of allegiance to the home country by the children born in another country, whatever may be their status in the land of birth, is an international practice still adhered to by most European nations—France, Italy, Germany, Switzerland, Greece. From this results what is called a "dual nationality" of a subject. In a country like the United States, where its Constitution endows children born therein with citizenship, the so-called "dual nationality" gives rise to an awkward situation in case its mother country adopts the military conscription system. To avoid this awkward situation, Japan enacted in the year 1916 a law which provides that a Japanese boy who has acquired a foreign nationality by reason of his birth in a foreign country may divest himself of Japanese nationality if his father, or other parental authority, takes the necessary steps to that end before he is fifteen years of age, or, if he has attained the age of fifteen, he may himself take the same steps, with the consent of his father or guardian, before he reaches the age of seventeen.[1] This law is objectionable because it fixes the age limit of expatriation at seventeen,

---

[1] For text of this law see Appendix K.

when the subject is yet a minor and is not competent to exercise his own choice. Fixing the age limit at seventeen is a provision in consonance with the Japanese military law, which imposes on all male Japanese subjects above that age the duty of military service. Consequently, all American-born Japanese males who have failed to expatriate before they have reached the age of seventeen are claimed as Japanese subjects and are subject to conscription, while at the same time they are American citizens. The existence of such a discordance in the laws and Constitution of the two countries has the possibility of giving rise to a serious international complication, and it seems advisable that some sort of settlement be made on this point between the American and Japanese Governments. The difficulty could, of course, be overcome if the Japanese parents who are determined to stay permanently in this country would take the necessary steps to expatriate their children as soon as they are born, or at the proper time. The hesitation they have heretofore manifested was greatly due to the uncertainty in which their future and that of their children was shrouded.

We cannot omit to emphasize in this connection the part which America can and has to perform. Of the numerous things America can do with profit we believe the task of Americanizing the Japanese to be the foremost. We wish to make it clear that, whether Japanese aliens are worthy or not, their children born in America are in any case Americans, and it is America's duty to make them worthy members of the nation. They are not foreigners or aliens, and, accordingly, it is clearly wrong, as well as unwise, to deal with them as if they were. Upon what we can do to guide the rising generation depends the future of the Japanese problem in America. This in turn must depend upon how America treats their parents. Disappearing gradually as they are, they are bequeathing their impressions and accomplishments to their children. Any generosity and kindness extended to them are acts not so much of altruism as of vital interest in the welfare of America herself, for they are the guardians of the Republic's sons and daughters of Japanese blood.

It is certainly not fair to slander and maltreat those people, who were originally brought in to fill the need of man-power and who have contributed much towards making the Pacific Coast what it is to-day. To prevent the influx of Japanese immigrants, to avoid the possible future development of difficult problems with Japan, there certainly ought to be some better means than gradually strangling the innocent people who individually are in no way to be blamed

for the present strained relations on the Pacific
Coast.

All these considerations lead us to a belief that
the time is now ripe for the American people, and
especially for the people of California, to reconstruct their attitude and policy towards the Japanese domiciled in this country. Every indication
seems to suggest that if, in place of the discriminatory policy so far resorted to with no better effect
than general irritation, a new policy be initiated, a
policy of constructive Americanization based upon
generosity, sympathy, and understanding, the
result will surely be far-reaching. It is a common
fact of human experience that one's attitude is
directly responded to by other people with whom
we deal. It was Thackeray, we believe, who said
that "the world is like a looking-glass; if we smile,
others also smile." What cannot be achieved by a
hostile policy is often easily and satisfactorily accomplished by sympathetic attitude and friendly
dealing. Give the Japanese the opportunity and
see what good use they will make of it.

We hardly need to reiterate that the Japanese-
California question—the main theme of this book
—is only a part of the vast problem which con-
fronts America and Japan. The present world
tendency is to bind increasingly all parts of the
world into one. The process of civilization, like a

revolving body, exerts centrifugal and centripetal force and gradually unifies all civilizations into a cohesive system. At present there are two centers of such forces, one in the East and another in the West, each trying to influence the other. By virtue of being the youngest and the most vigorous representatives of the two spheres, Japan and America, respectively, are naturally destined to shoulder together the great task of harmonizing and unifying these two great currents of human achievement. The task involves, from its gigantic nature, a great many difficulties and risks of which the present California issue is certainly one. All these difficulties must be squarely met and surmounted with courage and wisdom, since to shrink from the job is to commit the future relationship of the East and West to the cruel law of natural selection.

It is, however, generally true that the perfect understanding of the common aim settles the incidental difficulties arising in the process. This is particularly true in the case of the California-Japanese question, which is a partial issue of the great undertaking between America and Japan. The core of the California problem, our study has shown, is the question of assimilability of the Japanese. But what is the assimilation but the approach to the common standard of culture and ideals? The approach to the common standard of culture and ideals between the peoples of Asia and Europe and America is precisely the task in which Japan and the United States are engaged in unison. Herein is the explanation of our earlier assertion that the California problem is a miniature form of the problem of the East and West. Herein also is the support of our contention that to accelerate the coöperative effort of America and Japan for mutual understanding is the only and the best method of bringing about the solution of the Japanese problem in California or elsewhere in the United States. We wish, therefore, to emphasize once more that the wisest policy to follow in the future for America and Japan is not foolishly to sharpen the edge of swords for imaginary race wars, which are absurd, but to devote themselves wisely to learning and appreciating each other's accomplishments and greatness, from which alone true friendship can arise.

APPENDIX A

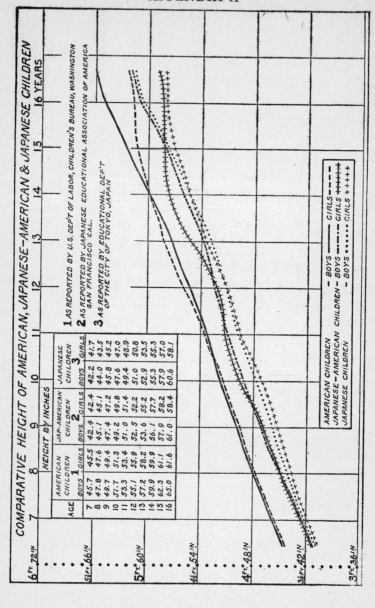

COMPARATIVE HEIGHT OF AMERICAN, JAPANESE—AMERICAN & JAPANESE CHILDREN

	AMERICAN CHILDREN 1		JAP-AMERICAN CHILDREN 2		JAPANESE CHILDREN 3	
AGE	BOYS	GIRLS	BOYS	GIRLS	BOYS	GIRLS
7	45.7	45.5	42.4	42.4	42.2	41.7
8	47.8	47.6	45.1	45.1	44.0	43.5
9	49.7	49.4	47.4	47.2	45.8	45.2
10	51.7	51.3	49.2	49.8	47.6	47.0
11	53.3	53.4	51.0	51.4	49.4	48.9
12	55.1	55.9	52.5	52.2	51.0	50.8
13	57.2	58.2	53.6	55.2	52.9	53.5
14	59.9	59.9	56.1	57.7	55.3	55.3
15	62.3	61.1	57.9	58.2	57.9	57.0
16	65.0	61.6	61.0	58.4	60.6	58.1

HEIGHT BY INCHES

1 AS REPORTED BY U.S. DEP'T OF LABOR, CHILDREN'S BUREAU, WASHINGTON

2 AS REPORTED BY JAPANESE EDUCATIONAL ASSOCIATION OF AMERICA SAN FRANCISCO CAL.

3 AS REPORTED BY EDUCATIONAL DEP'T OF THE CITY OF TOKYO, JAPAN

AMERICAN CHILDREN ——— BOYS ——— GIRLS ------
JAPANESE—AMERICAN CHILDREN — BOYS —·— GIRLS ++++++
JAPANESE CHILDREN — BOYS —·· GIRLS ······

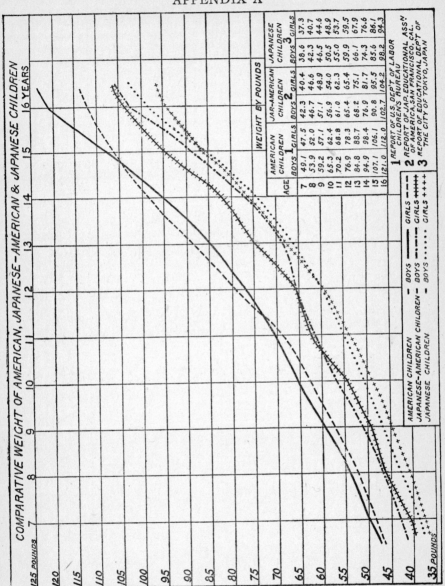

COMPARATIVE WEIGHT OF AMERICAN, JAPANESE—AMERICAN & JAPANESE CHILDREN

WEIGHT BY POUNDS

AGE	AMERICAN CHILDREN 1		JAP-AMERICAN CHILDREN 2		JAPANESE CHILDREN 3	
	BOYS	GIRLS	BOYS	GIRLS	BOYS	GIRLS
7	49.1	47.5	42.3	40.4	38.6	37.3
8	53.9	52.0	46.7	46.6	42.3	40.7
9	59.2	57.1	51.1	48.9	46.5	44.6
10	65.3	62.4	56.9	54.0	50.5	48.9
11	70.2	68.8	61.0	55.0	55.0	53.7
12	76.9	78.3	65.4	65.4	59.9	59.5
13	84.8	88.7	68.2	75.1	66.1	67.9
14	94.9	98.4	76.9	81.7	74.3	76.6
15	107.1	106.1	90.8	95.5	85.6	86.1
16	121.0	112.0	102.7	104.2	98.2	94.3

1 REPORT OF U.S. DEPT OF LABOR CHILDRENS BUREAU

2 REPORT OF JAP EDUCATIONAL ASSN OF AMERICA, SAN FRANCISCO CAL.

3 REPORT OF EDUCATIONAL DEPT OF THE CITY OF TOKYO, JAPAN

AMERICAN CHILDREN — BOYS ———— GIRLS ————

JAPANESE-AMERICAN CHILDREN — BOYS +++++ GIRLS +++++

JAPANESE CHILDREN — BOYS ————— GIRLS ••••••

125 POUNDS 120 115 110 105 100 95 90 85 80 75 70 65 60 55 50 45 40 35 POUNDS

16 YEARS 15 14 13 12 11 10 9 8 7

APPENDIX B

EXTRACTS FROM THE TREATY OF COMMERCE AND NAVI-
GATION AND PROTOCOL BETWEEN JAPAN AND THE
UNITED STATES OF AMERICA, OF FEBRUARY 21,
1911.

His Majesty, the Emperor of Japan, and the President of the United States of America, being desirous
to strengthen the relations of amity and good understanding which happily exist between the two nations,
and believing that the fixation in a manner clear and
positive of the rules which are hereafter to govern
the commercial intercourse between their respective
countries will contribute to this most desirable result,
have resolved to conclude a treaty of commerce and
navigation.

Article I.—The subjects or citizens of each of the
high contracting parties shall have liberty to enter,
travel, and reside in the territories of the other, to
carry on trade, wholesale and retail, to own or lease
and occupy houses, manufactories, warehouses, and
shops, to employ agents of their choice, to lease land
for residential and commercial purposes, and generally
to do anything incident to or necessary for trade, upon
the same terms as native subjects or citizens, submitting themselves to the laws and regulations there
established.

They shall not be compelled, under any pretext

whatever, to pay any charges or taxes other or higher than those that are or may be paid by native subjects or citizens.

The subjects or citizens of each of the high contracting parties shall receive, in the territories of the other, the most constant protection and security for their persons and property and shall enjoy in this respect the same rights and privileges as are or may be granted to native subjects or citizens, on their submitting themselves to the conditions imposed upon the native subjects and citizens.

Article IV.—There shall be between the territories of the two high contracting parties reciprocal freedom of commerce and navigation. The subjects or citizens of each of the contracting parties, equally with the subjects or citizens of the most favored nation shall have liberty freely to come with their ships and cargoes to all places, ports, and rivers in the territories of the other which are or may be opened to foreign commerce, subject always to the laws of the country to which they thus come.

Article V.—Neither contracting party shall impose any other or higher duties or charges on the exportation of any article to the territories of the other than are or may be payable on the exportation of the like article to any other foreign country.

Nor shall any prohibition be imposed by either country on the importation or exportation of any article from or to the territories of the other which shall not equally extend to the like article imported from or exported to any other country.

Article XIV.—Except as otherwise expressly provided in this treaty, the high contracting parties agree that in all that concerns commerce and navigation,

any privilege, favor, or immunity which either contracting party has actually granted or may hereafter
grant, to the subjects or citizens of any other State
shall be extended to the subjects or citizens of the
other contracting party . . . on the same or equiva-
lent conditions. . . .

Declaration

In proceeding this day to the signature of the treaty
of commerce and navigation . . . the undersigned
has the honor to declare that the Imperial Japanese
Government are fully prepared to maintain with equal
effectiveness the limitation and control which they
have for the past three years exercised in regulation of
the immigration of laborers to the United States.

(Signed) Y. UCHIDA.

February 21, 1911.

APPENDIX C

CALIFORNIA'S ALIEN LAND LAW

(Approved May 19, 1913)

The people of the State of California do enact as follows:

Section 1.—All aliens eligible to citizenship under the laws of the United States may acquire, possess, enjoy, transmit, and inherit real property, or any interest therein, in this State, in the same manner and to the same extent as citizens of the United States, except as otherwise provided by the laws of this State.

Section 2.—All aliens other than those mentioned in section one of this act may acquire, possess, enjoy, and transfer real property, or any interest therein, in this State, in the manner and to the extent and for the purposes prescribed by any treaty now existing between the Government of the United States and the nation or country of which such alien is a citizen or subject and not otherwise, and may in addition thereto lease lands in this State for agricultural purposes for a term not exceeding three years.

Section 3.—Any company, association, or corporation organized under the laws of this or any other State or nation, of which a majority of the members are aliens other than those specified in section one of this act, or in which a majority of the issued capital stock is owned by such aliens, may acquire, possess, enjoy, and convey real property, or any interest therein

204

in this State, in the manner and to the extent and for the purposes prescribed by any treaty now existing between the Government of the United States and the nation or country of which such members or stockholders are citizens or subjects, and not otherwise, and may in addition thereto lease lands in this State for agricultural purposes for a term not exceeding three years.

Section 4.—Whenever it appears to the court in any probate proceeding that by reason of the provisions of this act any heir or devisee cannot take real property in this State which, but for said provisions, said heir or devisee would take as such, the court, instead of ordering a distribution of such real property to such heir or devisee, shall order a sale of said real property to be made in the manner provided by law for probate sales of real property, and the proceeds of such sale shall be distributed to such heirs or devisee in lieu of such real property.

Section 5.—Any real property hereafter acquired in fee in violation of the provisions of this act by any alien mentioned in section two of this act, or by any company, association or corporation mentioned in section three of this act, shall escheat to, and become and remain the property of the State of California. The attorney general shall institute proceedings to have the escheat of such real property adjudged and enforced in the manner provided by section 474 of the Political Code and title eight, part three of the Code of Civil Procedure. Upon the entry of final judgment in such proceedings, the title to such real property shall pass to the State of California. The provisions of this section and of sections two and three of this act shall not apply to any real property hereafter acquired in the enforcement or in satisfaction of any lien now existing upon, or interest in such property, so long as such real property so acquired shall remain the property of the alien, company, association or corporation acquiring the same in such manner.

Section 6.—Any leasehold or other interest in real property less than the fee, hereafter acquired in violation of the provisions of this act by any alien mentioned in section two of this act, or by any company, association or corporation mentioned in section three of this act, shall escheat to the State of California. The attorney general shall institute proceedings to have such escheat adjudged and enforced as provided in section five of this act. In such proceedings the court shall determine and adjudge the value of such leasehold, or other interest in such real property, and enter judgment for the State for the amount thereof together with costs. Thereupon the court shall order a sale of the real property covered by such leasehold, or other interest, in the manner provided by section 1271 of the Code of Civil Procedure. Out of the proceeds arising from such sale, the amount of the judgment rendered for the State shall be paid into the State Treasury and the balance shall be deposited with and distributed by the court in accordance with the interest of the parties therein.

Section 7.—Nothing in this act shall be construed as a limitation upon the power of the State to enact laws with respect to the acquisition, holding or disposal by aliens of real property in this State.

Section 8.—All acts and parts of acts inconsistent or in conflict with the provisions of this act, are hereby repealed.

ALIEN LAND LAW

(Adopted November 2, 1920)

PROPERTY RIGHTS AND DISABILITIES OF ALIENS IN
CALIFORNIA

**Alien Land Law. Initiative Act. Permits Acquisition
and Transfer of Real Property by Aliens Eligible
to Citizenship, to Same Extent as Citizens Except
as Otherwise Provided by Law; Permits Other
Aliens, and Companies, Associations, and Corporations in Which they Hold Majority Interest,
to Acquire and Transfer Real Property Only as
Prescribed by Treaty, but Prohibiting Appointment Thereof as Guardians of Estates of Minors
Consisting Wholly or Partially of Real Property
or Shares in Such Corporations; Provides for
Escheats in Certain Cases; Requires Reports of
Property Holdings to Facilitate Enforcement of
Act; Prescribes Penalties and Repeals Conflict-
ing Acts.**

*An act relating to the rights, powers, and disabilities of
aliens and of certain companies, associations, and
corporations with respect to property in this State,
providing for escheats in certain cases, prescribing
the procedure therein, requiring reports of certain
property holdings to facilitate the enforcement of*

this act, prescribing penalties for violation of the provisions hereof, and repealing all acts or parts of acts inconsistent or in conflict herewith.

The people of the State of California do enact as follows:

Section 1.—All aliens eligible to citizenship under the laws of the United States may acquire, possess, enjoy, transmit, and inherit real property, or any interest therein, in this State, in the same manner and to the same extent as citizens of the United States, except as otherwise provided by the laws of this State.

Section 2.—All aliens other than those mentioned in section one of this act may acquire, possess, enjoy, and transfer real property, or any interest therein, in this State, in the manner and to the extent and for the purpose prescribed by any treaty now existing between the Government of the United States and the nation or country of which such alien is a citizen or subject, and not otherwise.

Section 3.—Any company, association or corporation organized under the laws of this or any other State or nation, of which a majority of the members are aliens other than those specified in section one of this act, or in which a majority of the issued capital stock is owned by such aliens, may acquire, possess, enjoy, and convey real property, or any interest therein, in this State, in the manner and to the extent and for the purposes prescribed by any treaty now existing between the Government of the United States and the nation or country of which such members or stockholders are citizens or subjects, and not otherwise. Hereafter all aliens other than those specified in section one hereof may become members of or acquire shares of stock in any company, association or corporation that is or may be authorized to acquire, possess, enjoy or convey agricultural land, in the manner and to the extent and for the purposes prescribed by any treaty now existing between the Government of the United States and the nation or country of which such alien is a citizen or subject, and not otherwise.

Section 4.—Hereafter no alien mentioned in section two hereof and no company, association or corporation mentioned in section three hereof, may be appointed guardian of that portion of the estate of a minor which consists of property which such alien or such company, association or corporation is inhibited from acquiring, possessing, enjoying or transferring by reason of the provisions of this act. The public administrator of the proper county, or any other competent person or corporation, may be appointed guardian of the estate of a minor citizen whose parents are ineligible to appointment under the provisions of this section.

On such notice to the guardian as the court may require, the superior court may remove the guardian of such an estate whenever it appears to the satisfaction of the court:

(*a*) That the guardian has failed to file the report required by the provisions of section five hereof; or

(*b*) That the property of the ward has not been or is not being administered with due regard to the primary interest of the ward; or

(*c*) That facts exist which would make the guardian ineligible to appointment in the first instance; or

(*d*) That facts establishing any other legal ground for removal exist.

Section 5.—(*a*) The term "trustee" as used in this section means any person, company, association or corporation that as guardian, trustee, attorney-in-fact

or agent, or in any other capacity has the title, custody
or control of property, or some interest therein, belonging to an alien mentioned in section two hereof, or to
the minor child of such an alien, if the property is of
such a character that such alien is inhibited from
acquiring, possessing, enjoying or transferring it.

(b) Annually on or before the thirty-first day of
January every such trustee must file in the office of the
Secretary of State of California and in the office of the
county clerk of each county in which any of the property is situated, a verified written report showing:

(1) The property, real or personal, held by him for
or on behalf of such an alien or minor;

(2) A statement showing the date when each item
of such property came into his possession or control;

(3) An itemized account of all expenditures, in-
vestments, rents, issues, and profits in respect to the
administration and control of such property with particular reference to holdings of corporate stock and
leases, cropping contracts, and other agreements in respect to land and the handling or sale of products
thereof.

(c) Any person, company, association or corporation
that violates any provision of this section is guilty of a
misdemeanor and shall be punished by a fine not exceeding one thousand dollars or by imprisonment in
the county jail not exceeding one year, or by both such
fine and imprisonment.

(d) The provisions of this section are cumulative
and are not intended to change the jurisdiction or the
rules of practice of courts of justice.

Section 6.—Whenever it appears to the court in any
probate proceeding that by reason of the provisions of
this act any heir or devisee cannot take real property

sought to be conveyed shall escheat to the State if the property interest involved is of such a character that an alien mentioned in section two hereof is inhibited from acquiring, possessing, enjoying or transferring it, and if the conveyance is made with intent to prevent, evade or avoid escheat as provided for herein.

A *prima facie* presumption that the conveyance is made with such intent shall arise upon proof of any of the following groups of facts:

(*a*) The taking of the property in the name of a person other than the persons mentioned in section two hereof if the consideration is paid or agreed or understood to be paid by an alien mentioned in section two hereof:

(*b*) The taking of the property in the name of a company, association or corporation, if the membership or shares of stock therein held by aliens mentioned in section two hereof, together with the memberships or shares of stock held by others but paid for or agreed or understood to be paid for by such aliens, would amount to a majority of the membership or the issued capital stock of such company, association or corporation;

(*c*) The execution of a mortgage in favor of an alien mentioned in section two hereof if said mortgagee is given possession, control or management of the property.

The enumeration in this section of certain presumptions shall not be so construed as to preclude other presumptions or inferences that reasonably may be made as to the existence of intent to prevent, evade or avoid escheat as provided for herein.

Section 10.—If two or more persons conspire to effect a transfer of real property, or of an interest therein, in violation of the provisions hereof, they are punishable by imprisonment in the county jail or State penitentiary not exceeding two years, or by a fine not exceeding five thousand dollars, or both.

Section 11.—Nothing in this act shall be construed as a limitation upon the power of the State to enact laws with respect to the acquisition, holding or disposal by aliens of real property in this State.

Section 12.—All acts and parts of acts inconsistent or in conflict with the provisions hereof are hereby repealed; *provided*, that—

(*a*) This act shall not affect pending actions or proceedings, but the same may be prosecuted and defended with the same effect as if this act had not been adopted;

(*b*) No cause of action arising under any law of this State shall be affected by reason of the adoption of this act whether an action or proceeding has been instituted thereon at the time of the taking effect of this act or not and actions may be brought upon such causes in the same manner, under the same terms and conditions, and with the same effect as if this act had not been adopted.

(*c*) This act in so far as it does not add to, take from or alter an existing law, shall be construed as a continuation thereof.

Section 13.—The legislature may amend this act in furtherance of its purpose and to facilitate its operation.

Section 14.—If any section, subsection, sentence, clause or phrase of this act is for any reason held to be unconstitutional, such decision shall not affect the validity of the remaining portions of this act. The people hereby declare that they would have passed this act, and each section, subsection, sentence, clause and phrase thereof, irrespective of the fact that any one or more other sections, subsections, sentences, clauses or phrases be declared unconstitutional.

APPENDIX E

CROPS RAISED BY JAPANESE AND THEIR ACREAGE.

Product.	Total Acreage of Cultivation.	Acreage by Japanese.	Percentage of Japanese Cultivation Against Total Cultivation.
Berries	6,500	5,968	91.8
Celery	4,000	3,568	89.2
Asparagus	12,000	9,927	82.7
Seeds	20,000	15,847	79.2
Onions	12,112	9,251	76.3
Tomatoes	16,000	10,616	66.3
Cantaloupes	15,000	9,581	63.8
Sugar Beets	102,949	51,604	50.1
Green Vegetables	75,000	17,852	23.8
Potatoes	90,175	18,830	20.8
Hops	8,000	1,260	15.7
Grapes	360,000	47,439	13.1
Beans	592,000	77,107	13.0
Rice	106,220	16,640	15.6
Cotton	179,860	18,000	10.9
Corn	85,000	7,845	9.2
Fruits, Nuts	715,000	29,210	4.0
Hay, Grain	2,200,000	15,753	0.0

Reported by the Japanese Agricultural Association of California, 1919.

APPENDIX F

ALIEN JAPANESE ADMITTED TO CONTINENTAL UNITED STATES.

Year.	No. of Japanese Immigrants.	Year.	No. of Japanese Immigrants.
1869	63	1891	1,136
1870	48	1892	1,498
1871	78	1893	1,380
1872	17	1894	1,931
1873	9	1895	1,150
1874	21	1896	1,110
1875	3	1897	1,526
1876	4	1898	2,230
1877	7	1899	3,395
1878	2	1900	12,626
1879	4	1901	4,908
1880	4	1902	5,325
1881	11	1903	6,990
1882	5	1904	7,771
1883	27	1905	4,319
1884	20	1906	5,178
1885	49	1907	9,948
1886	194	1908	9,544
1887	229		
1888	404		
1889	640		
1890	691		

Year.	Admitted.	Departed.	Balance.
1909	2,432	5,004	−3,411
1910	2,498	5,024	−3,472
1911	4,282	5,869	−1,587
1912	5,358	5,437	− 79
1913	6,771	5,647	+1,124
1914	8,462	6,300	+2,162
1915	9,029	5,967	+3,062
1916	9,100	6,922	+2,178
1917	9,159	6,581	+2,578
1918	11,143	7,691	+3,452
1919	11,404	8,328	+3,076
1920	12,868	11,662	+1,206

In the above, the figures for 1869–1891 are adopted from the reports of the United States Superintendent of Immigration; those for 1892–1908, from Immigration Commission Report Vol. 23, p. 5; those for 1909–1920, from the Report of Commissioner General of Immigration.

APPENDIX G

JAPANESE ADMITTED INTO CONTINENTAL UNITED STATES:
ARRIVALS AND DEPARTURES.

Year.	Number of Arrivals.	Departed.	Total Gains Up to Date.
1861–1870	218		
1871–1880	149	25,000	
1881–1890	2,270	(estimated)	
1891–1900	20,829		
1901–1910	54,838		
1911–1920	87,576	70,404	
Total......	165,880		
No. of transient immigrants from Hawaii.........	15,000 (estimated)		
Total......	180,880	95,404	87,476

APPENDIX H

IMMIGRANTS AND NON-IMMIGRANTS.

Year.	Total Number Admitted.	Immigrants.	Non-Immigrants.	Percentage of Non-Immigrants Against Total Number Admitted.
1909	2,432	675	1,757	72.2
1910	2,498	589	1,909	76.4
1911	4,282	726	3,556	83.0
1912	5,358	894	4,464	83.3
1913	6,771	1,371	5,400	79.7
1914	8,462	1,762	6,700	79.2
1915	9,029	2,214	6,815	75.5
1916	9,100	2,958	6,142	67.5
1917	9,159	2,838	6,321	69.0
1918	11,143	2,604	8,539	76.6
1919	11,404	2,278	9,126	80.0
1920	12,868	3,682	9,186	70.1

Official figures of Commissioner General of Immigration.

APPENDIX I

DISTRIBUTION OF JAPANESE AND CHINESE POPULATION IN THE UNITED STATES.

DISTRIBUTION OF JAPANESE POPULATION.

Census.	1880	1890	1900	1910
Total United States....	148	2039	24,326	72,157
New England.........	14	45	89	272
Middle Atlantic.......	27	202	446	1,643
East North Central....	7	101	126	482
West North Central....	1	16	223	1,000
South Atlantic........	5	55	29	156
East South Central....	...	19	7	26
West South Central....	...	42	30	428
Mountain............	5	27	5,107	10,447
Pacific..............	89	1,532	18,296	57,703

DISTRIBUTION OF CHINESE POPULATION.

Census.	1880	1890	1900	1910
United States........	105,465	107,488	89,863	71,531
New England.........	401	1,488	4,203	3,499
Middle Atlantic.......	1,277	4,689	10,490	8,189
East North Central....	390	1,254	2,533	3,451
West North Central....	423	1,097	1,135	1,195
South Atlantic........	74	669	1,791	1,582
East South Central....	90	274	427	414
West South Central....	758	1,173	1,555	1,303
Mountain............	14,274	11,572	7,950	5,614
Pacific..............	87,828	85,272	59,779	46,320

Taken from Gulick, *American Democracy and Asiatic Citizenship*, pp. 152, 177.

APPENDIX J

DISTRIBUTION OF JAPANESE IN UNITED STATES.

(According to Consular Division as Reported by Foreign Department, Japan.)

Districts.	Male.	Female.	Total for 1919.
Seattle.............	14,568	4,397	18,965
Portland...........	5,829	1,637	7,466
San Francisco......	37,375	16,578	53,953
Los Angeles........	22,644	9,861	32,505
Chicago...........	2,336	378	2,714
New York.........	3,320	284	3,604
	86,072	33,135	119,207

APPENDIX K

Article XVIII.—When a Japanese, by becoming the wife of a foreigner, has acquired the husband's nationality, then such Japanese loses her Japanese nationality.

Article XX.—A person who voluntarily acquires a foreign nationality loses Japanese nationality. In case a Japanese subject, who has acquired foreign nationality by reason of his or her birth in a foreign country has domiciled in that country, he or she may be expatriated with the permission of the Minister of State for Home Affairs. The application for the permission referred to in the preceding paragraph shall be made by the legal representative in case the person to be expatriated is younger than fifteen years of age. If the person in question is a minor above fifteen years of age, or a person adjudged incompetent, the application can be made with the consent of his or her legal representative or guardian. A stepfather, a stepmother, a legal mother, or a guardian may not make the application or give the consent prescribed in the preceding paragraph without the consent of the family council. A person who has been expatriated loses Japanese nationality.

Article XXIV.—Notwithstanding the provisions of the preceding six articles a male of full seventeen years or upwards does not lose Japanese nationality, unless he has completed active service in the army or navy, or he is under no obligation to enter into it. A person who actually occupies an official post—civil or military—does not lose Japanese nationality notwithstanding the provisions of the foregoing seven articles.

Article XXVI.—A person who has lost Japanese nationality in accordance with Article XX may recover Japanese nationality provided that he or she possesses a domicile in Japan, but this does not apply when the person mentioned in Article XVI has lost Japanese nationality. In case the person who has lost Japanese nationality in accordance with the provision of Article XX is younger than fifteen years of age, the application for the permission prescribed in the preceding paragraph shall be made by the father who is the member of the family to which such person belonged at the time of his expatriation; should the father be unable to do so, the application shall be made by the mother; if the mother is unable to do so, by the grandfather; and if the grandfather is unable to do so, then by the grandmother.

APPENDIX L

A MINUTE OF HEARING AT SEATTLE, WASHINGTON,
BEFORE THE HOUSE SUB-COMMITTEE ON
IMMIGRATION AND NATURALIZATION

DIRECT EXAMINATION

July 27, 1920.
Evening Session
SEATTLE

JAMES SAKAMOTO, produced as a witness, having
been first duly sworn, testified as follows:

QUESTIONS BY MR. BOX:

Q. What is your name?
A. James Sakamoto.
Q. Where do you live?
A. 1609 Yesler Way.
Q. You were born in the United States?
A. Yes, sir.
Q. Where were you born?
A. In Seattle, Washington.
Q. Right here?
A. Yes.
Q. Are you full of Seattle spirits?
A. You bet.
Q. You only refer to one kind. How old are you?
A. Seventeen. I was born in 1903; March 22d.

Q.   You go to school here?

A.   Oh, yes.

Q.   In the high school?

A.   The Franklin High.

Q.   About how many boys are there here in and about Seattle that were born here, along about your age, from three or four years younger to two or three years older?

A.   Well, I only know of the fellows that I associate with. I can't tell you the fellows that I don't know about.

Q.   Do you know a number?

A.   I don't know many of them.

Q.   A half a dozen?

Q.   How many in your high school are Japanese boys?

A.   I think I am the only one.

Q.   Are there many young ladies? Do you know this young lady that just testified?

A.   Yes, sir.

Q.   Are there many such nice looking girls as she is in Seattle?

A.   You better ask them.

Q.   You get along all right in school?

A.   Oh, yes, sir.

Q.   You don't have any trouble with your classes, and boys?

A.   I have lots of fun.

Q.   You have a good time?

A.   Yes, sir.

Q.   Did you attend the Japanese Language School?

A.   Yes, sir; eight years.

Q.   What did they teach you there?

A.   Taught me Japanese.

Q. The Japanese language?

A. Yes, sir.

Q. Did they teach you Japanese history?

A. I wasn't able to learn very quick.

Q. You were not very quick to learn, but they **did** that, teach the history of Japan?

A. They tried to.

Q. Didn't they succeed with a boy as bright as you are, going to high school?

A. They were successful, but I did not succeed. See?

Q. You read the Japanese language now?

A. I can't read it; it is too hard.

Q. You really can't read any?

A. There are three different kinds of words and letters. I can read the easiest.

Q. In other words, you have adopted the road of least resistance with the Japanese language?

A. Sure.

Q. You talk Japanese with your parents?

A. In a simple, broken language.

Q. Do they talk English?

A. They can't talk English. They have been here quite long, but they have never had a chance to talk English.

Q. Let me ask you this; do you get along very well with them?

A. In my home?

Q. Yes.

A. Sure. They are my father and mother.

Q. (Mr. Siegel.) And you say that you don't understand the Japanese language sufficiently well to carry on a conversation with them?

A. I understand them, but that is about all.

Q. How do they arrange to get along with you, if you can't speak the language orally?

A. They just about guess what I am trying to tell them.

Q. In other words, you are always asking for money. Is that the principal idea?

A. May be, not any more, but I used to.

Q. When they talk to you, you understand them all right?

A. Oh, yes; I understand them.

Q. (Mr. Raker.) Would you tell us why, you haven't, or didn't, and haven't given more attention and worked harder to become familiar with the Japanese language and history?

A. That is a hard question to ask me just now.

Q. I know it is, but I think you know, my boy; tell us in your own language, in your own way?

A. Well, suppose we go to school five hours a day, the American school. We attend Japanese school for two hours; that is overwork two hours, you see, and we don't get paid for over time.

Q. I guess you are about pretty near right, didn't I? You are the kind of a fellow that is going to be thinking a little about money as you grow up, and you are going to make it in Seattle.

A. I haven't got a business.

Q. (Mr. Raker.) What I was asking that question for, I am going to put it direct. I want you to give me your good frank answer, which I know you will. Is it your determination when you get a little older, and begin to think over the situation, that you want to become familiar with the English language and understand the American ways rather than to devote your time to Japanese ways and language?

A. Well, I want to be an American more than a Japanese. I was born here.

Q. That is one of the reasons you haven't devoted your time to the Japanese language. How old were you when you started?

A. I started the same year when I went to Grammar School.

Q. That was when?

A. Five years old. Five years old I started to kindergarten, and at six I started to Grammar School.

Q. So when you started to kindergarten did you start in the Japanese School?

A. No, when I was six.

Q. And you did that from the time you were six until you were fourteen?

A. I think that is right, fourteen.

Q. How old are you now?

A. Seventeen.

Q. You have to renounce the Japanese Emperor before you are seventeen?

A. I don't know a thing about it.

Q. You know, don't you, that you are claimed as a citizen by Japan, and also by the United States.

A. I don't care. I was born here.

Q. Is it your intention to remain an American citizen or be a Japanese citizen?

A. Why shouldn't I remain an American? I was born here. Why should I go back there? This is my home here.

Q. You intend to remain an American citizen?

A. Nobody is going to stop me.

Q. That's what I want to get at. Do you remember when you were first told that you were a native-born American citizen; do you remember when that was first told you?

A. I don't know.

Q. How long have you felt the pride that you are a young American citizen? How long have you held that feeling of pride?

A. Since I went to Grammar School.

Q. Has every young Japanese boy here expressed that feeling as you do to us; have you heard them talk about it?

A. They don't talk about it much. It is mostly their home training. My father and mother don't care whether I am an American. They would rather have me an American.

Q. And they have encouraged you to be an American?

A. Sure.

Q. And your teachers have?

A. Oh, yes, naturally.

Q. And you like the idea?

A. Sure.

Q. Your father and mother intend to remain here all their lives, do they, as far as you know?

A. Well, I would like to have them go back and see their home once again, but that is about all. I don't know what I can do.

Q. (Mr. Vaile.) As far as you know, their own intention is to live here, except for a visit home, perhaps, the rest of their lives?

A. Yes, sir.

Q. Suppose you visit Japan. You know, don't you, that the Japanese Emperor still claims you as his subject? Suppose you are required to render military service to Japan, what would be your position on that subject?

A. It would be a pretty difficult one, but I will get out of it.

Q. Following that, suppose you were required to render military service to the United States, what will be your position?

A. I will get in.

Q. Exactly. We are glad to meet you. Good luck to you.

(*Witness Excused.*)

APPENDIX M

COMPARATIVE STANDING OF INTELLIGENCE AND BE-
HAVIOR OF AMERICAN-BORN JAPANESE CHILDREN
AND AMERICAN CHILDREN DISCUSSED BY SEVERAL
PRINCIPALS OF ELEMENTARY SCHOOLS OF LOS
ANGELES, CALIFORNIA.

*Request Sent to the Board of Education of Los Angeles,
California.*

December 24, 1920.

President of the
    Board of Education,
    Los Angeles, California.

MY DEAR SIR:

I am collecting data on the intellectual and moral
status of American-born Japanese children. Among
the data the most important, I need hardly say, are
their school records.

I shall highly appreciate your courtesy if you will be
pleased to provide me with the valuable information
you have at your command bearing on the subject.
What I am particularly interested in is the average
record of American-born Japanese children and its
comparison with the record of American children.

Yours very respectfully,

(Signed) T. IYENAGA.

Method of Gathering Material

December 31, 1920.

DEAR MR. SHAFER:

May I trouble you to select two of your schools in which you have the largest Japanese attendance and secure for me at your earliest possible convenience data as to the number of Japanese children in those schools and the points about them that are touched upon in the accompanying letter?

My thought is this—that if we secure records from two or three schools where we have the largest Japanese attendance, this will suffice as a basis for decision as to the other such schools.

MRS. DORSEY.

January 7, 1921.

Mrs. Adda Wilson Hunter, *Principal*, Moneta School, Miss Mary A. Colestock, *Principal*, Hewitt St. School, Miss Mary A. Henderson, *Principal*, Amelia St. School, Miss Lizzie A. McKenzie, *Principal*, Hobart Blvd. School.

A communication has been received from Dr. T. Iyenaga stating that he is collecting data on the intellectual and moral status of American-born Japanese children. He is anxious to know the average record of American-born Japanese children in the schools and how it compares with the record of American children.

Will you kindly send me statement concerning the results in your schools?

Very truly yours,
Assistant Superintendent.

Replies

(1)

Office of the Principal of Hewitt St. School, District No. 151

Report of American-born Japanese Children.

January 17, 1921.

MY DEAR MR. SHAFER:

The American-born Japanese children, who are enrolled in this school, compare most favorably with the American children both intellectually and morally. They are like all groups of children. We find some very bright children and some very dull ones. As a whole, they are more persevering and more dependable than the class of white children found in this school.

Miss Oliver, who has been working with the Japanese for the past four years, said, "When with them I feel that I am in the company of well-bred Americans."

Truly yours,

MARY A. COLESTOCK,

Prin.

(2)

Amelia St. School, City

January 19, 1921.

MR. HARRY M. SHAFER,
  Assistant Superintendent,
  Los Angeles City Public Schools,
  Los Angeles, California.

DEAR MR. SHAFER:

My general observation has been that given anything of an equal chance, children are children, human nature is human nature, and brains are brains—whatever the mother tongue may be. Compared with our other foreign children, or with other children born in America of foreign parentage not Japanese, keeping in mind the differences in social position that exist in all classes, whatever the nationality may be, I cannot see much difference along any line between our Japanese children and our Mexicans, our French and our Italians; nor do I think any of them differ radically from what we are apt to term "American" children. Few families are many generations away from some foreign ancestors. . . .

Our Japanese children are called brighter and more studious, sometimes, than the others. I think this is due to the fact that they have, in many cases, ambitious, educated parents who follow school work up very closely in the home. Where home restrictions are lifted, such conditions do not always prevail, any more than in cases of other neglected children. *They must* be studious. Discipline of American-born Japanese children is not so close in the home as it seems to be with children born in Japan and reared along Japanese lines, yet such children show much more initiative in all of their work at school. They catch the American spirit.

As summary, I would say that physically, mentally, morally, given the same chance, there does not seem to me to be a great difference among children of the different nationalities, but this difference is most readily noticed. The other nationalities do assimilate quickly, and lose, to a great extent, their parents' national traits in short time; but it is exceedingly hard to get the same results with our Japanese children. They cling to one another, to their own ways, and to their own language, even after many years of work in public schools, where most social barriers are broken down. My personal feeling in the matter is that this condition is the result of lack of American education in the Japanese homes and lack of American touch with the Japanese mothers.

Our Home teachers are doing much to help along this line, but it is slow work, and work that takes much time, and requires great tact on part of the workers.

Most important to me is the work our public schools are doing with the Japanese girls, the mothers of to-morrow.

Yours respectfully,

MARY A. HENDERSON.

(3)

Report of Intellectual and Moral Status of American-born Japanese Children

MONETA SCHOOL, LOS ANGELES SCHOOL DIST.

As a rule American-born Japanese children know no English when entering school. Their progress at first, therefore, is more slow than that of English speaking children. Japanese children require one year to complete one half year's work through the first, second, and third grades. After the third grade they complete the work in the time assigned.

They are especially good in handwork. Their chief difficulty is with English. In application they rank high.

As to their moral status they are neither better nor worse than other children.

MRS. ADDA WILSON HUNTER,
Principal Moneta School.

January 14, 1921.

Report of Intellectual and Moral Status of American-Born Japanese Children

Grade.	Amer.-Born Japanese Enrolled.	Time to Complete Work of ½ Year.	Standard Age of Grade.	Average Age of Am.-Born Jap'se.	Rank in Class.	Application.	1. In What Do They Excel? 2. What is Greatest Drawback?
Kgn.	13	1 yr.	4½–6	5		Good	1. Handwork. 2. Do not speak English.
B-1	21	1 yr.	6–7			Good	1. Drawing, writing, handwork. 2. Do not speak English.
A-1	4	1 yr.	6–7	9		Good	1. Handwork. 2. Do not speak English.
B-2	2	1 yr.	7–8	9		Good	1. Handwork. 2. Do not speak English.
A-2	3	1 yr.	7–8	10		Good	1. Handwork. 2. Do not speak English.
B-3	2	5 mos.	8–9	10	Excel.	Poor	1. Spelling, arithmetic. 2. English.
A-3	3	1 yr.	8–9	10	Fair	Good	1. Spelling, arithmetic. 2. English.
B-4	1	5 mos.	9–10	9	Excel.	Excel.	1. Arithmetic. 2. English.
A-4	1	5 mos.	9–10	11	Excel.	Excel.	1. Arithmetic, spelling. 2. English.
B-5	2	5 mos.	10–11	11	Excel.	Excel.	1. Arithmetic, spelling. 2. English.
B-6	2	5 mos.	11–12	10	Good	Excel.	1. History, geography. 2. Arithmetic.
A-6	1	5 mos.	11–12	12½	Excel.	Excel.	1. Arithmetic, history. 2. Geography.

(4)

HOBART BLVD. SCHOOL,
LOS ANGELES, CALIFORNIA,
January 13, 1921.

MR. HARRY M. SHAFER,
Assistant Supt. City Schools.

MY DEAR MR. SHAFER:

In reply to your inquiry relative to the American-born Japanese pupils of our school, I enclose statement as to results noted in the various classes.

Trusting that this may serve the purpose desired, and appreciating your very kindly interest,

Sincerely,

LIZZIE A. MCKENZIE,
Principal.

Hobart Blvd. School.   January 13, 1921.

Report on Japanese Pupils
(American-born)

Many of the Japanese fail in First Grade on account of inability to understand the English language. In succeeding grades, progress is satisfactory as shown by the following tabulation of current date:

Enrolled.		To Be Promoted.	Enrolled.		To Be Promoted.
B-1	16	10	A-3	1	1
A-1	7	6	B-4	2	2
B-2	5	5	A-4	0	
A-2	4	4	B-5	2	1
B-3	1	1	A-5	1	1
			B-6	1	1
			A-6	0	

Total enrolled, 40.
Total promoted, 32.

We find these children as a rule clever in use of pen and crayon, possessing light touch, having correct ideas of form, and excellent taste in selection of color.

As pupils they follow direction well, and are usually free from faults of rudeness or improper language. Of the forty above Kindergarten, three are troublesome and are persistent cases. In general, it may be said that these children as a class compare favorably with others in matters of progress and of conduct as well.

LIZZIE A. McKENZIE,
Principal.

LITERATURE ON THE SUBJECT

Books

ANNALS OF AMERICAN ACADEMY OF POLITICAL AND SOCIAL SCIENCE, January, 1921. *Present Day Immigration with Special Reference to the Japanese.*

ANNALS OF AMERICAN ACADEMY OF POLITICAL AND SOCIAL SCIENCE, September, 1909. *Chinese and Japanese in America.*

GULICK, SYDNEY L. *American Democracy and Asiatic Citizenship.* Scribners, New York, 1918. *The American-Japanese Problem.* Scribners, New York, 1914.

ICHIHASHI, Y. *Japanese Immigration.* Marshall Press, San Francisco, 1915.

KAWAKAMI, K. K. *American-Japanese Relations.* Revell, New York, 1912. *Asia at the Door.* Revell, New York, 1914. *Japan in the World Politics.* Revell, New York, 1917.

MASAOKA, N. (Editor). *Japan to America.* G. P. Putnam's Sons, New York, 1915.

MILLIS, H. A. *The Japanese Problem in the United States.* McMillan, New York, 1915.

PITKIN, WALTER B. *Must We Fight Japan?* The Century Co., New York, 1921.

RUSSELL, LINDSAY (Editor). *America to Japan.* G. P. Putnam's Sons, New York, 1915.

SCHERER, J. A. A. *The Japanese Crisis.* Stokes, 1915.

THE JAPANESE-AMERICAN NEWS. *The Japanese-American Year Book*, 1910 and 1918. San Francisco.

OFFICIAL PUBLICATIONS

Annual Reports of the United States Commissioner-General of Immigration.

Bureau of Labor (California). Biennial Reports, and especially, "Report on the Japanese in California."

California and the Oriental. Report of California State Board of Control, with Governor Wm. D. Stephens's letter addressed to Secretary of State Bainbridge Colby. California State Printing Office, Sacramento, 1920.

Department of Commerce, Bureau of Census. Chinese and Japanese in the United States, 1910. Bulletin 127, Washington Printing Office, 1914.

Immigration Commission. Changes in Bodily Form of Descendants of Immigrant. Senate Document, No. 208, 61st Congress, 2nd Session. Washington Government Printing Office, 1910.

Immigration Laws of the United States. (Revised Federal Statutes).

KAHN, CONGRESSMAN. Japanese-California Problem. Congressional Record, 60, 4 : 78–82, December 9, 1920.

METCALF, SECRETARY. Report on the Japanese School Question.

Naturalization Laws of the United States. (Revised Federal Statutes.)

Reports of the Immigration Commission. Immigrants in the Industries, Vols. 23, 24, 25, Senate Document, No. 633, 61st Congress.

ROOSEVELT, THEODORE. Presidential Message to Congress, 1907. House of Representatives; Message of the President of the United States, and Accompanying Documents. Part I; pp. 492–846. Ex. Doc. No. 1.

PAMPHLETS

CALIFORNIA FARMERS' CO-OPERATIVE ASSOCIATION. *Japanese Immigration and the Japanese in California*, 1919.

CLEMENT, E. W. *Expatriation of Japanese Abroad.* Japanese Association of America, San Francisco, 1916.

ELIOT, CHAS. W. *Friendship between the United States and Japan.* Japanese Merchants' Association, Portland, Oregon.

GADSBY, JOHN. *Foreign Land-Ownership and Leasing in Japan*, 1920. Japanese Association of America, San Francisco, 1914.

GULICK, SYDNEY L. *How Shall Immigration be Regulated?* 1920. *Japan and the Gentlemen's Agreement.* 1920. *The New Anti-Japanese Agitation.* 1920.

ICHIHASHI, Y. *Japanese Immigration, Its Status in California.* 1913.

IRISH, JOHN P. *Campaign of Lies, Stolen Letters of Senator Phelan.* 1920. *Shall Japanese-Americans in Idaho be Treated with Fairness and Justice or Not?* 1921.

KAWAKAMI, K. K. *Senator Phelan, Dr. Gulick and I.* Bureau of Literary Service, San Francisco, 1920.

LAMONT, THOMAS, AND OTHERS. *Japan.* 1920.

PEOPLE'S LEAGUE OF JUSTICE. *Petition by People's League of Justice*, Los Angeles, California, 1920.

REA, GEORGE BRONSON. *Japan's Right to Exist.* *Far Eastern Review*, Shanghai, China, 1920.

ROOSEVELT, T. *America and Japan.* Reprint from the New York *Times.*

SHIMA, GEORGE. *An Appeal to Justice.* 1920.

TAFT, HENRY W. *Our Relations with Japan.* Japan Society, New York, 1920.

THE AMERICAN COMMITTEE OF JUSTICE. *California and the Japanese.* Oakland, California, December, 1920.

TYNDALL, PHILIP. *Proposed Initiative Measure to be Presented to the Legislature of 1921*, Seattle, Washington.

VANDERLIP, FRANK. *Mr. Vanderlip's Message.*

WALLACE, J. B. *Waving the Yellow Flag in California.* Reprinted from the Dearborn *Independent.*

WILLIAMS, B. H. *The Case against the Japanese.* 1920.

ARTICLES IN PERIODICALS

"America and the Japanese Relations." WAINWRIGHT, S. H. *Outlook*, 124 : 392, March, 1920.

"America's Responsibility on the Pacific." GREENBIE, S. *North American Review*, 212 : 71–79, July, 1920.

"Another Japanese Problem." McLEOD, H. *New Republic*, 24 : 184–6, October 20, 1920.

"Anti-Japanese Agitation." *Business Chronicle*, 9, 18 : 137–49, September, 1920.

"Asia's American Problem." ROBINSON, GEROID. *Pacific Review*, 367–388, December, 1920.

"California and the Japanese." KAWAKAMI, K. K. *Nation*, 112 : 173–174, February 2, 1921.

"California and the Oriental." The Letter of WM. D. STEPHENS to the Secretary of State Colby. *The Pacific Review*, 349–361, December, 1920.

"California-Japanese Problem." *The Pacific Voice*, 5, 10 : 4–10.

"California-Japanese Question." WOOLSEY, THEODORE S. *The American Journal of International Laws*, Oxford Press, 15, 1 : 24–26, January, 1921.

"Co-operation between Japan and America." KANEKO, K. *Japan Review*, 24–26, December, 1920.

"Discrimination against the Japanese." *New Republic*, 24 : 135–6.

"Future of Japanese-American Relations." SHIDEHARA, K. *Japan Review*, 170–171, April, 1920.

"Hegemony of the Pacific." *Living Age*, 316 : 638–40.

"Japan, a Great Economic Power." LONGFORD, J. H. *Nineteenth Century*, 523 : 526–39, September, 1920.

"Japan and America." *Far Eastern Review*, 16 : 335–36.

"Japan and the United States, a Suggestion." OTTO, M. C. *Japan Review*, 334–336, October, 1920.

"Japan and the Japanese-California Problem." IYENAGA, T. *Current History*, 13, 1 : 1–7, October, 1920.

"Japan as Colonizer." *Stead's Review*, 53, 7 : 358–9.

"Japan Challenges Us to Control California." STODDARD, L. *World's Work*, 40 : 48–85.

"Japan Our New Customer." STARRETT, W. A. *Scribner's*, 66 : 517–18.

"Japan's Diplomacy of Necessity." *Living Age*, 316: 638–640.

"Japan's New Difficulties with China." *The New*

York Times Current History, 457–458, December, 1920.

"Japan's Use of Her Hegemony." FERGUSON, J. C. *North American Review*, 210 : 456–459.

"Japan's Aggression." INMAN, J. M. *Forum*, 65, 1 : 1–9, January, 1921.

"Japanese-American Relations." SHIDEHARA, K. *Outlook*, 125 : 317–18, June 16, 1920.

"Japanese-American Relations." YOSHINO, SAKUZO. *Pacific Review*, 418–421, December, 1920.

"Japanese and the Pacific Coast." RYDER, R. W. *North American Review*, 213, 1 : 1–15, January, 1921.

"Japanese Farmers' Contribution to California." CHIBA, TOYOJI. *Japan Review*, 212–13, May, 1920.

"Japanese Imperialism in Siberia." CHAMBERLAIN, W. H. *Nation*, 110 : 798–9.

"Japanese in America." TRENT, P. J. *Review of Reviews*, 61 : 76–8, June, 1920.

"Japanese in California." BRIGGS, A. H.; JOHNSON, H. B.; LOOFBOUROW, I. J. *Japan Review*, 166–170, April, 1920.

"Japanese in California." IRISH, JOHN P. *Japan Review*, 7–72, January, 1920.

"Japanese in California." JORDAN, D. S. *The Pacific Review*, 316–65, December, 1920.

"Japanese Issue in California." STODDARD, L. *World's Work*, 40, 5 : 585–600, September, 1920.

"Japanese Language Schools." KAWAKAMI, K. K. *Japan Review*, 14–15, January, 1921.

"Japanese Problem in California." LOCAN, C. A. *Current History*, 13 : 7–11, October, 1920.

"Japanese Pupils and American Schools." FULTON, C. W. *North American Review*, December, 1906.

"Japanese Question." KAWAKAMI, K. K. *Pacific Review*, 365–78, December, 1920.

"Japanese Views of California." *Literary Digest*, 67, 1 : 20–1.

"Japanthropy." WOOLSTON, H. B. *Pacific Review*, 289–96, December, 1920.

"Legal Aspects of the Japanese Question." McMurray, Orrin K. *Pacific Review*, 396–403, December, 1920.

"Liberalism in Japan." DEWEY, JOHN. *Dial*, 63 : 283–5; 335–7; 369–71.

"Light on the Japanese Question." KINNEY, H. W. *Atlantic Monthly*, 126 : 832–42, December, 1920.

"Moral Factors in Japanese Policy." BLAND, J. O. P. *Asia*, 211–217, March, 1920.

"Oriental Immigration from the Canadian Standpoint." BAGGS, THEODORE H. *Pacific Review*, 408–418, December, 1920.

"Oriental in California." IRISH, JOHN P. *Overland*, 75 : 332–3, April, 1920.

"Oriental Problem, as the Coast See It." HART, J. A. *World's Work*, March, 1906.

"Oriental Question and Popular Diplomacy." PRUETT, ROBERT L. *Japan Review*, 291–92, August, 1920.

"'Possum and the Dinosaur." MASON, G. *Outlook*, 125 : 319–20, June 16, 1920.

"Race Prejudice: Psychological Analysis." SATO, K. *Japan Review*, 237–238, June, 1920.

"Shall East and West Never Meet?" SATO, K. *Japan Review*, 336–37, October, 1920.

"Some Aspects of the So-called Japanese Problem." VANDERLIP, F. A. *Outlook*, 125 : 380–4.

"What are the Japanese Doing towards Americanization?" SASAMORI, JUNZO. *Japan Review*, 22–24, December, 1920.

"What Japan Wants." ADACHI, K. *Nation*, 181–82, Feburary 2, 1921.

"When East is West." GULICK, SYDNEY L. *Outlook*, 102 : 12–14, April 3, 1920.

INDEX

Adaptability, Japanese disposition of, 20
Æsthetic temperament of Japanese, 13
Age distribution of Japanese in California, 112
Agreement, Root-Takahira, 34
Agriculture, Japanese, in California, 120–147; causes of Japanese progress in, 123–126
Ainu, 14
American-born Japanese, 174–177
American disposition, 9
Americanization, criterion of, 151–154
Ancestors, Japanese, 16
Anti-Alien Land Laws, 138–142; effect of, 145; Appendixes C, D
Anti-Japanese Agitation, causes of, 75–89
Asiatic policy, Japan's, 33–45
Assimilation, 137; 148–177; and nationalism, 148–159; meaning of, 151–154; biological, 155–162; of Japanese immigrants, 168–174
Australia, Japanese emigration to, 64–67

Birth-rate of Japanese in California, 109–119
Boas, Professor, quoted, 163
Bolsheviki, 38
Buddhism, 25
Bushido, 15, 21

California, causes of Anti-Japanese agitation in, 75; causes of Japanese influx to, 50–63; Christianity among Japanese in, 169–170; competition in, 133–135; congestion of Japanese in, 87–89; cultural assimilation of Japanese in, 166–168; genesis of hostility towards Japanese in, 71; population of, 93; problem, 7
Canada, Japanese emigration to, 67–69
Capitalism, 29
Castle, Professor, quoted, 159
Chiba, T., quoted, 129
China, Japan's coöperation with, 42–45
Chinese, 23, 95
Chivalry, proletarian, 21
Christianity, 28
Colonization, Japanese policy of, 18
Confucianism, 25, 27
Congressional sub-Committee on Immigration and Naturalization, 176
Constitution, Japanese, 11

Democracy, industrial, 31
Democratic institutions, Japanese training in, 172
Den Do Dan, 169–170
Despotism, Japanese, 22
Dewey, Professor John, 29
Dispersal of Japanese in California, 189
Disposition, Japanese, 20
Dual nationality, 191

East and West, 4, 195–196

Economic status of Japanese in California, 171
Education, system of, 31
Emotional nature, of Japanese, 9
English, Japanese ability to command, 170
Eta, 18
Eurasiatic relationship, 6
Expatriation Law of Japan, Appendix K

Farmers, Japanese, in California, 132–138
Fishberg, Dr., quoted, 164

"Gentlemen's Agreement," 100–106
German, influence on Japan, 30; idealism, 32
Gikyoshin, 21
Group consciousness of Japanese, 16
Gulick, Dr. Sydney L., quoted, 157

Hara kiri, 12
Hearn, Lafcadio, 44
Hedonism, Japanese, 15
Hideyoshi, 10
History of Japanese, 10, 20
Humanism, 32

Immigration to
  Australia, 64–67
  Canada, 67–69
  South America, 69
  United States, 69–75
Industrial democracy, 31
Intelligence of Japanese in California, 170
Intermarriage, 155–162

Japan, topographical conditions of, 13; Nature of, 14
Japan's, Asiatic Policy, 33; land area, 52; agriculture, 52–55; industry, 57–62; population, 55–57; social conditions, 62–63
Japanese, ability to speak English, 170; age distribu-
tion of, in California, 112; agriculture in California, 120–147; ancestors, 16; assimilability of, 148–177; birth rate in California, 109–119; civilization of, 14; Constitution, 11; death rate of, in California, 117; descendants in California, 164–166, 174–177; economic status of, in California, 171; farm labor, 126–131; farmers in California, 132–138; immigration to America, 97–107; Land Laws, 142–145; morality of, in California, 168–169; nationality, 85–86; number of, in California, 91; philosophy, 24; sex distribution of, in California, 112; social system, 30; susceptibility of, 12; training in civics, 172
Jesuit Fathers, 10
Jones and East, quoted, 159

Kikotsu, 21
Kipling, quoted, 4
Kojiki, 16
Korea, amalgamation of, 34; local self-government in, 36; situation in, 35–37
Koreans, 18
Kusama, Shiko, note, 170

Labor, 30
Land, amount held by Japanese in California, 135–137
Land Laws, Anti-Alien, 138–142; Appendixes C and D
League of Nations, 19
Lippman, Walter, note, 86

Manchuria, 37
Mankind, 6
Marriage, Japanese, 11
Millis, Professor H. A., quoted, 157
Morality of Japanese in California, 168–169
Morris, Roland, 186
Myth, 17

Nationalism, 148
Native-born Japanese, 174
Nevada, 23
Newlands, U. S. Senator, 23
Nihongi, 16
Nitobé, Dr., 22
Number of Japanese in California, 91

Oakesmith, John, quoted, 176
Occidental learning, 26
Occidentalism, ultra, 19
Otokodate, 21

Pacific Coast, 193–194
Passports, 103
Patriotism of Japanese, 17
Perry, Commodore, 3
Philosophy, Japanese, 24
Picture brides, 113
Political rights of Japanese, 31
Politics as a cause of agitation, 80–82
Population of Japanese in California, 90–97
Positivism, English, 28
Pragmatism, 29, 32
Pride of Japanese, 11, 19
Propaganda, 83

Race war, 7
Racial difference, 83–85
Radicals, Japanese, 20
Relationship, American Japanese, 7
Roosevelt, Theodore, 33
Root-Takahira Agreement, 34
Russo-Japanese war, 18

Sakura, Sogoro, 22
Samurai, 12, 15

San Francisco Chamber of Commerce, 187
Santayana, 29
Science, lack of, in Japan, 15
Sex distribution of Japanese in California, 113
Shantung, 39
Shibusawa, Viscount, 186
Smuggling of Japanese to United States, 107–109
Social, force, 23; *milieu* as affecting man, 165; reorganization, 29
South America, Japanese emigration to, 69
State Board of Control of California, 96
Stephens, Governor, quoted, 5, 23, 122
Suicide in Japan, 12

Thought, Japanese, 29
Tokugawa régime, 22
Traits, Japanese, 9
Treaty, American-Japanese, 187, Appendix B

United States, the, Japanese immigration to, 69–74
Unity, national, 17
Utilitarians, 29

Vanderlip, Frank, 187

Wang Yang Ming, 26
White and yellow races, 5
Wilson, Woodrow, quoted, 154
Women, status of Japanese, 31

Yamato race, 14
"Yellow peril," 82
Young Japan, 14

*A Selection from the
Catalogue of*

G. P. PUTNAM'S SONS

❧

**Complete Catalogues sent
on application**

An Introduction to The History of Japan

By

Katsuro Hara

"At last we have a concise and readable history of Japan by a native scholar who does not begin either in the ages of eternity or at 660 B. C. . . . In a word, he is a modern Japanese, who in the spirit of the age writes in an honest way. Casting aside the inveterate insular prejudices belonging to a people long in hermitage, he tells what is known. In a word, he illustrates handsomely his own country's proverb, 'Proof is better than argument.' . . . The spirit of this well arranged and indexed volume is discerned in the penultimate paragraph: 'What we aspire to earnestly as our national ideal is to make our country able to stand shoulder to shoulder with the senior Western nations in contributing to the advance and welfare of world civilization.'"

DR. WILLIAM E. GRIFFIS
in the *New York Herald*

G. P. Putnam's Sons

New York   **London**

The Story of Japan

By
David Murray, Ph.D., LL.D.
Late Advisor to the Japanese Minister of Education

Crown Octavo *Fully Illustrated*

No. 38 in "The Story of the Nations"

"Little seems omitted that would be of value in giving a clear and rational picture of the nation 'at home,' as one may say. The account of the Shogun rule is a very interesting one, and is ably disentangled from the complicated circumstances that have so often placed it in a false light." *New York Times.*

G. P. Putnam's Sons

New York **London**